P

# Managing Your Learning

This book is about analysing, understanding and managing the way you learn. Whether you are working towards a formal qualification, are undertaking work-related training or are learning informally by yourself, *Managing Your Learning* will help you to assess and build on your strengths, and identify and deal with your weaknesses.

You can use this book by yourself, or in an organised group or class. There are 25 sections, each containing:

- A diagnostic questionnaire on a specific aspect of learning

- Key points to explore

- Suggestions for further action

Each chapter has sections for you to make notes about your own situation, and there is advice on study problems and study skills. By the end of the book, you will have developed an individual learning profile and worked out a personal action plan.

**Geoffrey Squires** is a Reader in Education and leads the Educational Development Team at the University of Hull. He has taught courses on 'learning to learn' for many years.

E BOOK VERSION AVAILABLE

# MANAGING YOUR LEARNING

Geoffrey Squires

London and New York

First published 2002 by Routledge
11 New Fetter Lane, London EC4P 4EE

Simultaneously published in the USA and Canada
by Routledge
29 West 35th Street, New York, NY 10001

Reprinted 2003 (twice)

*Routledge is an imprint of the Taylor & Francis Group*

© 2002 Geoffrey Squires

Designed and typeset in Officina and Novarese by
Keystroke, Jacaranda Lodge, Wolverhampton
Printed and bound in Great Britain by
St Edmundsbury Press Ltd, Bury St Edmunds, Suffolk

*British Library Cataloguing in Publication Data*
A catalogue record for this book is available from the British Library

*Library of Congress Cataloguing in Publication Data*
A catalog record for this book has been requested

ISBN 0–415–23765–3

# Contents

## Part C: Processes 85

## Part D: Outcomes 129

# Preface

This book has grown out of the various courses on 'learning to learn' which I have run over the years, and my main debt is to those people who came on them, from whom I learned a great deal. I would also like to thank the various teachers, lecturers, trainers, students and trainees in this region who worked through earlier drafts and whose comments were invaluable in helping me to produce this final version. Further comments from readers are always welcome.

It is impossible to write a book of this kind that will meet every individual interest and need. However, I hope that the framework set out here will help people to reflect on their own learning, to begin a conversation with themselves about it, and to share their insights with others.

Geoffrey Squires
Hull

# HOW TO USE THIS BOOK

This book is about analysing and managing the way you learn. In particular, it should help you to pinpoint and overcome any problems you are having. It is aimed at people over 16 who have finished their compulsory education, and assumes that you have already started a new education or training course or an informal learning project of your own.

You can use the book by yourself, with friends, or in an organised group or class. It will take you about three hours to work through it. The book breaks down learning into 25 different aspects and by exploring each of these you will gradually build up a profile of your own learning. You can then develop an individual action plan.

Although the book contains plenty of practical advice, there are no quick fixes here. Learning is not like that. It involves many different aspects of you and your environment, and only by understanding these can you really learn how to manage your learning. So each of the 25 sections follows the same pattern: first there is a short questionnaire which explores your responses, then a list of key points which you need to relate to your own situation, and then some suggestions about what you might do.

Don't try to complete the whole book in one go; give yourself time to back off and think about it, and if necessary return to some sections later. Indeed, you can use the book several times over a period of months or years, since your own learning situation may well change during that time.

A few basic symbols have been used to guide you through the book, as follows:

📖 follow these instructions

✉ write your own notes here

⇨ read this list

* refer to the Notes and Further Reading at the end

You can use a highlighter to mark anything you feel is particularly relevant to you. This will help you make the book your own. Write your personal notes in the shaded spaces provided and use a pad if you need more room.

Turn now to the next page for **Instructions** on using the book.

# 📖 Instructions

The book is divided into four parts and 25 sections. To use it, you need to follow five basic steps.

## 📖 Step One

Read the introduction to Part A. Then go to **Course** (Section 1) and you will find five statements about it. Respond to each one by ringing it as follows:

− (minus) if you mainly or completely disagree

? (query) if your response is 'partly' or you are not sure

+ (plus) if you mainly or completely agree

If a statement doesn't apply to you, leave it blank.

## 📖 Step Two

Add up your responses, counting +1 for each plus, −1 for each minus, and nothing for queries or blanks. Subtract the minuses from the pluses, and put the total in the space below: it could range from −5 to +5.

## 📖 Step Three

If your total is +3 or more, go straight on to the next section. If your total is anything less than +3, turn over the page and read the **Key Points**. Then make any **Personal Notes** you want about how these points apply to you, or anything else you think is important. Then read the suggestions on possible **Action**, and note down any that you could follow up in the space headed **What should I do?**

## 📖 Step Four

Move on to the next section and repeat the process until you reach the end of that part of the book. Take a break at that point, and think about how it is going. Look back at some of the sections where your score was +3 or more. Even if you had no particular problems there, they will help you get a fuller picture of the way you learn.

## 📖 Step Five

When you have finished all the sections, turn to the **Profile** at the back of the book and follow the instructions there on completing it and the **Action Plan**. You will also find some other **Notes**, **Tips for the Terrified** and a **Study Skills Index** near the end of the book.

# 📖 Choosing your Questionnaire

There are five versions of the questionnaire. Choose the one that suits you best, as follows:

**SIXTH FORM**
if you are doing AS/A levels or other post-GCSE courses in school sixth forms or sixth form colleges. Students in the Scottish and Republic of Ireland systems can also use this version, provided they do a little bit of translating and substitute 'Highers' or 'Leaving Cert.' where necessary.

**FURTHER EDUCATION**
if you are doing a course in a further education or technical college, such as NVQs, GNVQs, BTEC/EDEXCEL, City and Guilds, LCC, etc. If you are doing A levels, use the Sixth Form version.

**HIGHER EDUCATION**
if you are a full-time or part-time undergraduate, or taking intermediate qualifications such as certificates and diplomas. If you are from overseas, you will need to bear in mind cultural differences between your system and the UK one.

**TRAINING AND DEVELOPMENT**
if you are undergoing initial or continuing training and professional development in or outside your organisation or profession. This version covers both the public and private sector. Since a lot of work-related learning is informal, it may be useful in some cases to have a look at the Informal Learning version as well.

**INFORMAL LEARNING**
A lot of learning takes place independently outside the formal education or training systems. If you have been involved in this kind of informal learning (which might relate to your family, work, leisure or other activities) this is the version for you. However, since informal learning differs from taught courses, the questionnaire takes a different form, so please read the special instructions below before starting.

If you are studying at a distance or by **open learning**, you can still use the book but you will need to adapt some parts of it in your own mind to suit your particular situation.

**Adult education** students should use the **Further Education** or **Higher Education** version depending on the level of the course, though some of the sections (for example on assessment) may not apply fully.

**Teachers and trainers** can integrate the book into a more general, organised programme of study support or learning development; see the **Notes for Staff** at the end.

Learning is a very individual matter, and you will need to use your common sense in working through the book. The words that are used may not be quite the ones you are familiar with. Not everything that is said will necessarily apply to you. You should cross-check with the advice your teachers or trainers give you, particularly in terms of assessment, where they will be in the best position to judge.

Even if you get low scores in some sections, this does not always mean that there are problems, merely that you need to think about the issues. Above all, what you do about your learning is up to you. No book, and probably no other person, can make your decisions for you. You will need to think through, and perhaps discuss with other people, how you want to change your approach.

---

### Another Way

If you don't fancy doing too much reading right away, complete all the questionnaires and fill in the Profile first. Talk to somebody about it if you can. Then go back to the sections that you need to or want to. Take one at a time and spread the work over a couple of weeks. That way you will gradually cover all the important bits.

---

Finally, please note that the following words are used in a particular way in the book:

**Course** means the whole programme or course that you are doing. Particular subjects, modules or units are referred to as **parts** of a course.

**Teacher** covers anyone responsible for teaching or training in any form, and so includes all tutors, lecturers, trainers, instructors and supervisors.

**Learner** refers to anyone involved in organised learning on a taught course, and so covers students, trainees, apprentices and staff undergoing professional development. It also includes people who are learning informally on their own.

**Work** means your studies, not your job.

**Assessment** refers to anything that leads to a mark or grade, and so covers all kinds of examinations, assignments, tests, projects and so on.

Before you begin, **make a few notes** on what you want to get out of the book. What are your main problems? How would you like to manage your learning better?

✉  Personal Notes

Now turn to Part A (page 1) and begin.

# 📖 Special Instructions on Informal Learning

Informal learning takes place outside any taught or organised course, so we need to approach it differently from the other four questionnaires. It is very common: people teach themselves all sorts of things at all ages, though often they are not conscious of this, and don't actually think of it as 'learning'. Often they just regard it as a normal part of their work, life or leisure.

So the first step is to identify some examples of informal learning you have undertaken sometime during the last three years. These may have been related to your work (paid or unpaid), your home or family, your leisure interests and activities, your social responsibilities or roles, or your personal development and relationships. It may take you a while to think of examples, but once you start, you will probably realise that you have done more informal learning than you thought.

We will call each of these examples a 'learning project' even though you may not have thought of it like that. The basic criteria are that you should have spent the equivalent of at least ten hours in all on a 'learning project' (and perhaps a lot more) and developed your knowledge and skills to the point where you could have passed them on to someone else (and perhaps did).

✉ **Note down three examples below.**

Project 1

What was it about? ...........................................................................
Why did I start it?...........................................................................
How long did I spend on it?...........................................................
Over what period of time? .............................................................

Project 2

What was it about? ...........................................................................
Why did I start it?.............................................................................
How long did I spend on it?...............................................................
Over what period of time? .................................................................

Project 3

What was it about? ...........................................................................
Why did I start it?.............................................................................
How long did I spend on it?...............................................................
Over what period of time? .................................................................

Now choose one project to work through the book. The questionnaire will refer to your 'learning project' and you will have to adapt some of what is said in each section to fit your informal context. (If you want, you can skip Sections 2, 5, 10, 16 and 22 since these relate mainly to taught courses, though it is interesting to compare the two kinds of learning situations.) Your questionnaire is in the past tense because it is about learning that you have already completed, but if you want to choose an ongoing project, that's fine. The word **informal** is always in bold in the text to draw your attention to it. The points on **informal** learning are usually at the end of each list, but do look at the other points as well, since many of them will be relevant to you. And every time you read the word 'course' think 'project'.

When you have worked through all the sections and completed the profile, you can go back to your second example and do the same again, using the spaces in the margin. Learning projects often vary a good deal, and a second one may throw up different issues. As an **informal** learner, you will probably be able to manage the process quite well already, but this analysis will help you to reflect on it more systematically than you may have done before.

# PART A: BASICS

This first part explores the basic aspects of your learning situation: what you are learning, what resources you have available, how you are coping, what the teaching or training is like, and so on. We go into some of these topics in more detail later in the book but it is important to get the general picture first.

📖 Remember that if your score is less than +3, you should work through the whole section, otherwise you can go straight on to the next one.

📖 When you have finished **Learning** (Section 6), stop and think about how it is going. Are you clear about what you are doing? If not, please read the instructions again. Do your scores seem realistic? Are you getting at any problems that exist? Are you being critical and self-critical enough?

📖 And before going on to Part B, look back at some of the sections where you scored +3 or more, making any notes you want. These will help to give you a fuller picture of your learning.

# 1 Course
## what you are learning

**Sixth Form**

1a. I am glad I chose the subjects I am doing.      − ? +
1b. The subjects I am doing are the right ones for me.      − ? +
1c. I can cope with this level of work.      − ? +
1d. Each subject is turning out as I expected.      − ? +
1e. I am enjoying each of the subjects.      − ? +

         Total

**Further Education**

1a. I am glad I chose the course I am doing.      − ? +
1b. The course I am doing is the right one for me.      − ? +
1c. The course is pitched at the right level for me.      − ? +
1d. The course is turning out as I expected.      − ? +
1e. I am enjoying the course.      − ? +

         Total

**Higher Education**

1a. I am glad I chose the course I am doing.      − ? +
1b. The course I am doing is the right one for me.      − ? +
1c. I can cope with undergraduate work.      − ? +
1d. The course is fulfilling my expectations.      − ? +
1e. I am enjoying the course.      − ? +

         Total

**Training and Development**

1a. I am glad I am doing this training programme.      − ? +
1b. The programme I am doing is the right one for me.      − ? +
1c. The programme is pitched at the right level for me.      − ? +
1d. The programme is meeting my needs.      − ? +
1e. I am enjoying the training programme.      − ? +

         Total

**Informal Learning**

1a. I am glad I embarked on my learning project.      − ? +
1b. My learning project was the right one for me.      − ? +
1c. I coped with the demands of my learning project.      − ? +
1d. I learned what I expected to learn through my project.      − ? +
1e. I enjoyed my learning project.      − ? +

         Total

# COURSE

## Key Points

- This first section is about the match or mismatch between you and what you are learning.

- There are two sides to the match. The first is you. How do you see yourself as a student or trainee? What interests you? What are your own personal aims or goals? We often have a mixture of goals.

- How confident are you that you can cope with this level or type of work? What are your own strengths and weaknesses? Do you think you are better at some subjects or topics than others?

- The other side of the match is the course. Is it what you thought it was going to be? Does it cover what you expected? Is it pitched at the right level for you? Do you like the style of teaching/training? Do you feel comfortable on the course?

- Any surprises?

- Perhaps some parts of the course are OK but not others. If so, what is the difference? Is it to do with the content or the way it is taught? Or something else again?

✉ **If there are major differences between the different parts of your course, make a brief note of them here.**

- How much choice did you have anyway? Did you make the decision to enrol on the course or did others advise you or decide for you? Or did you just drift into it? Were there timetable clashes?

- If you feel there is a mismatch between you and the course, is it perhaps teething trouble, something that may sort itself out over time? What stage are you at in the course? Is it early days yet?

- If you learned something **informally**, outside a taught course, the same kinds of questions arise. Did you choose the right kind of topic or project? Obviously, it was your choice, but we don't always know what we are letting ourselves in for. How does it look now with hindsight?

If you feel there is some kind of mismatch between you and what you are learning, it is important to try to sort it out, since it may affect many of the other aspects covered in this book. Make some notes below on how these points relate to you and your situation, and anything else you think is important here.

✉  Personal Notes

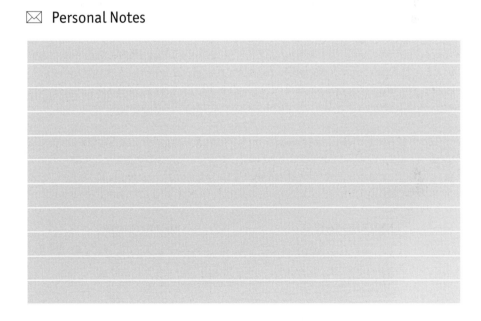

## Action

If you only have **initial worries** about the match between you and your course, it may be best to stick with it. It is quite normal to experience some anxieties at the beginning of a new course, since it is likely to be strange and unfamiliar in various ways: not just the content, but the people running it and doing it. Give yourself a chance to **settle down**.

It is quite common to prefer some parts of a course to others, but if you do, try to work out why. Make a list of **likes and dislikes**. This may tell you something about yourself as well as the course.

If you have **serious doubts**, then it is important to talk to someone about them. The most obvious people are those directly involved (the teachers, lecturers or trainers) because they may be familiar with the problems and have come across them before. They can also tell you how the course is going to progress and whether things are likely to change. Although there are sometimes pressures on staff to keep up enrolments, most teachers and trainers prefer not to have people on their courses who don't really want to be there. There may also be central **advisory services** for students which can help you.

If you don't feel you can approach the staff, then try to **find someone else who will listen** to your problems. (That may or may not include family.) Friends or colleagues can often help, since they will know you even if they don't know much about the course.

If your course is part of a training and development programme, you may need to talk to the **person responsible for staff development** in your organisation, since it should be tied into that process. However, employees sometimes get sent on courses which are not right for them for all sorts of reasons.

A more systematic way of approaching the situation is to do a **SWOT** analysis. Divide a page into four sections, and write down all the Strengths, Weaknesses, Opportunities and Threats that relate to the decision. Leave it for a day, and you will probably think of a few more to add. Then try to analyse the situation.

| STRENGTHS | WEAKNESSES |
|---|---|
| | |
| | |
| | |
| | |

| OPPORTUNITIES | THREATS |
|---|---|
| | |
| | |
| | |

If you think you lack the basic knowledge and skills to do the course, make sure you look at **Foundations** (Section 14) later. If you think the course does not suit your style of learning, look at **Meta-learning** (Section 24) when you come to it.

Find out if there are **choices later in the course**. Some courses begin with a common, compulsory core, which then opens up into pathways or options. For example, you might have some choice in terms of assignments, projects or modules, and this could make it easier to match the course with your own preferences.

If you do plan to withdraw from the course, **check out any consequences** this might have. For example, if you are getting financial support such as a grant or loan, will it affect that? Will it have any consequences for your work or job? You will also need to think through the alternatives. What else might you do? Is it possible to switch to another course? If so, when?

If you think you have embarked on the wrong **informal** learning project, don't just carry on with it as a matter of pride. Choose something which is more appropriate.

Now make notes below on what you can do about this first aspect of your learning.

## ✉ Course: what should I do?

# 2 Induction
## finding your way

**Sixth Form**

| | | | | |
|---|---|---|---|---|
| 2a. I know what to expect in each of my subjects. | − | ? | + | |
| 2b. I know what is expected of me in each of my subjects. | − | ? | + | |
| 2c. I know how to approach each subject. | − | ? | + | |
| 2d. I understand the difference between GCSEs and this level of work. | − | ? | + | |
| 2e. I could explain to new students what each subject involves. | − | ? | + | |
| | | | | Total |

**Further Education**

| | | | | |
|---|---|---|---|---|
| 2a. I know what to expect on my course. | − | ? | + | |
| 2b. I know what is expected of me on my course. | − | ? | + | |
| 2c. I know how to approach my course. | − | ? | + | |
| 2d. I understand the difference between GCSEs and this course. | − | ? | + | |
| 2e. I could explain to new students what this kind of course involves. | − | ? | + | |
| | | | | Total |

**Higher Education**

| | | | | |
|---|---|---|---|---|
| 2a. I know broadly what to expect on my course. | − | ? | + | |
| 2b. I know generally what is expected of me on this course. | − | ? | + | |
| 2c. I know how to approach the work on this course. | − | ? | + | |
| 2d. I understand the difference between A levels and higher education. | − | ? | + | |
| 2e. I could tell new students what to expect in higher education. | − | ? | + | |
| | | | | Total |

**Training and Development**

| | | | | |
|---|---|---|---|---|
| 2a. I know what to expect on this training programme. | − | ? | + | |
| 2b. I know what is expected of me on this training programme. | − | ? | + | |
| 2c. I know how to approach the work on this programme. | − | ? | + | |
| 2d. I think I know the ropes on this programme. | − | ? | + | |
| 2e. I could brief a new participant about the programme. | − | ? | + | |
| | | | | Total |

**Informal Learning**

| | | | | |
|---|---|---|---|---|
| 2a. I knew broadly what my learning project would involve. | − | ? | + | |
| 2b. I knew roughly what demands my project would make. | − | ? | + | |
| 2c. I knew how to set about my learning project. | − | ? | + | |
| 2d. I foresaw the kinds of problems my project would throw up. | − | ? | + | |
| 2e. I could advise someone starting on a project like mine. | − | ? | + | |
| | | | | Total |

# INDUCTION

## Key Points

- This section is about finding your way into and around a new course.

- A course is a complex thing. It involves structures, regulations, timetables, materials, processes, people. Some introduction or induction into these is necessary.

- With a short course or workshop, a five-minute introduction may be all that is needed. With longer courses, induction is often a more elaborate process, involving pre-course information, presentations, discussions and social events. The important thing is that you understand what will be involved and how you should approach it.

- However, formal introductions do not always work well. The presentations can be stiff and the meetings awkward. There may be information overload. As a newcomer, you may feel shy or afraid to ask questions.

- Also, induction may not tell you much about the less formal aspects of the course, what is sometimes called the hidden curriculum.* How much work is actually involved? How are you really expected to behave? What are the 'rules of the game'? And how much say have you in the whole process?

REMINDER: *an asterisk refers to the* **Notes and Further Reading** *at the back of the book, which you can turn to for more information.*

- Another problem is that if one course follows on from another, staff may simply assume that everyone knows the ropes and may not bother with any introduction. Misunderstandings may come to light only later. This is a particular danger where courses are consecutive, running on from one year or stage to the next.

- If you come from overseas you may experience some 'culture shock' in the system. This can also happen with older students who come back into education or training after a long gap. Things may be very different from what they remember!

- Previous students or participants often provide an informal kind of induction, through the grapevine. Where staff tell you about the course, participants tell you about the staff. However, this information is not always reliable: things may have changed, or the person may have had a particularly good or bad experience.

- People seem to differ in the amount of induction they need. Some of us want the complete map from the very beginning, and feel insecure if we don't have it; others are happy if they just know what they have to do the next day. What about you?

- The basic question is: *do you know what you are getting into*? If not, why not? And how can you find out?

- If there are different stages or options on a course or programme, you may want some induction and guidance at each one. You need to get your bearings not just at the start of the voyage, but throughout.

Now write down some thoughts on how this applies to you.


## ✉ Personal Notes

# Action

If you were given materials about the course (prospectuses, handbooks, information sheets, outlines, etc.) have you **read them properly**? They may contain answers to some of your questions which you could not absorb at the time.

Are there any **taster sessions** which would allow you to sample different parts of the course?

If there are members of staff who are responsible for advising you (**supervisors or tutors**) you could approach them with any questions. They will expect you to do so at the beginning of a course, and should welcome queries at any time.

However, if this seems too formal or you can't get hold of them, you can often approach **the teachers/trainers who are running your particular classes or sessions**. Don't ask them just as they are about to start; wait until the end when they have finished and are tidying things up. It is often easier to talk to staff with whom you already have a working relationship. After a while, you will get a sense of which members of staff are more approachable than others.

If you feel a bit confused or at sea, try **spending more time with other participants**, at breaks or after sessions. People often chat about what they are doing on the course, and you will pick up a good deal this way.

During each class or session, **listen for any hints or cues that staff give out**, particularly about forthcoming work or assessment. You can ask for a list of assessment tasks and deadlines early on.

If an **official curriculum or syllabus** exists, you can try to get hold of a copy, though this will usually only give you the bare bones, and some staff are defensive about making such information available, perhaps because they feel it may be misinterpreted.

**Previous participants** can be a useful source of information, but don't rely totally on what they say, for the reasons mentioned earlier.

**Don't worry *too* much about the long term**. Learning is often an unfolding or evolutionary process, and things which you do not understand now may become clearer as you go on.

If you are an **informal** learner you have to provide your own induction! However, you may be able to find people who have already done what you are planning to do, and **pick their brains**. Ask around. Use your contacts and networks.

Now make some notes on what you might do.

✉ Induction: what should I do?

# 3 Resources

## what you need

**Sixth Form**

3a. I have all the materials, equipment and facilities I need.     −   ?   +
3b. I have access to all the learning resources I need in each
    subject.                                                        −   ?   +
3c. The learning resources are good.                               −   ?   +
3d. Nothing prevents me using these learning resources.            −   ?   +
3e. I make good use of the school's/college's learning resources.  −   ?   +

                                                                   [        ] Total

**Further Education**

3a. I have all the materials, equipment and facilities I need.     −   ?   +
3b. I have access to all the resources I need for my course.       −   ?   +
3c. The learning resources are good.                               −   ?   +
3d. Nothing stops me using these learning resources.               −   ?   +
3e. I make good use of the college's learning resources.           −   ?   +

                                                                   [        ] Total

**Higher Education**

3a. I have all the materials, equipment and facilities I need.     −   ?   +
3b. I have access to all the learning resources necessary for my
    course.                                                        −   ?   +
3c. The university's learning resources are good.                  −   ?   +
3d. There are no barriers to my use of the learning resources.     −   ?   +
3e. I make good use of the university's learning resources.        −   ?   +

                                                                   [        ] Total

**Training and Development**

3a. I have all the materials, equipment and facilities I need.     −   ?   +
3b. I have access to all the learning resources I need for my
    programme.                                                     −   ?   +
3c. The learning resources are of a high quality.                  −   ?   +
3d. There are no barriers to using these resources.                −   ?   +
3e. I make good use of the available learning resources.           −   ?   +

                                                                   [        ] Total

**Informal Learning**

3a. I had everything I needed for my learning project.             −   ?   +
3b. I was able to find all the materials, equipment and facilities I
    wanted.                                                        −   ?   +
3c. The resources I had available were good.                       −   ?   +
3d. There were no problems with learning resources on my project.  −   ?   +
3e. I made good use of the available resources.                    −   ?   +

                                                                   [        ] Total

# RESOURCES

## Key Points

- One of the benefits you should get from doing a course is the 'wherewithal' for learning: all the handouts, materials, books, software and equipment you need. New technology plays an increasing part in teaching and learning.

- These resources will obviously vary from course to course and subject to subject. Science and technology courses require a lot of equipment; drama, hairdressing, catering or agriculture courses each need their own kinds of facilities. In other cases, books or articles will still form the main resource.

✉ **What are the main kinds of resources needed in your field? Make a brief note of them here.**

- The first question is whether these learning resources are adequate for your course and your needs. Are there enough of them?

- Are the materials of good quality, and pitched at the right level for you? Are they comprehensive and up-to-date?

- Even if they exist, can you get at them? Are they restricted in terms of time and place? Are there peaks in demand when you can't get hold of a book or can't get lab space or a place at a computer terminal? Are there quiet study areas?

- If you are expected to provide some of these resources yourself, is cost a problem for you? If so, can you get help with such expenses?

- If you are part-time, is access more difficult than for full-timers? If you study at a distance, can you get hold of all the materials and resources you need?

- Have you got adequate access to email and the internet? The first may be important in keeping in touch both with teachers and others doing the course. The second opens up a vast range of materials, though the quality varies enormously and you have to be very selective. Do you know how to make use of these facilities?

- If you are an **informal** learner, you have to get hold of all these learning resources for yourself. Sometimes other people can help in advising you what you need and how to find it, though you will still have to spend time tracking stuff down and deciding whether it is what you actually want.

- Finally, how good are you at making use of all these resources? Do you have the necessary skills to get the best out of them? And do you spend enough time on them? Having the resources available is one thing, using them fully is another.

Which of these points apply to you?

## ✉ Personal Notes

# Action

Learning resources depend ultimately on **budgets**, so a lot of this may be out of your hands. However, if you feel that the resources are seriously lacking in some way, the best plan is to **get together with some other students or trainees** and put the case to those in charge. There may be staff–student committees for just this. In any case, you will achieve more as a group than individually. Staff may well be sympathetic, though they will often be limited in what they themselves can do.

Sometimes the problems will be simply down to **poor organisation and lack of thought**. If you think that some staff are lazy or sloppy in providing good learning materials, make your views known, again preferably in a group. There is no excuse for this, since it is part of their responsibility. But be positive: come with a well-thought-out list of points and present it in terms of helping to improve the course as a whole.

Support staff, such as **librarians, technicians and secretaries**, are often good sources of information. They tend to know where things are.

Be on the look-out for **second-hand resources**. You may be able to pick up books or manuals from previous years' students, but be wary in fields such as law or other professional domains where it is essential to have the up-to-date text. Keep an eye out for special deals on computers, either in the national press or through a students' union.

If there are **peaks in demand for library and computer facilities**, you need to think and plan ahead, and not leave everything to the last minute when everyone else will be wanting to use them too.

**WARNING:** back up all your computer material regularly (software can usually be reinstalled but data will be lost). Systems do crash, and there are many viruses around these days.

Your institution may run **short courses on library and computing skills**, and it is worth taking advantage of these, since such skills are useful well beyond your course. But **friends** or colleagues can also be a major resource in showing you how to do things. And then you can help someone else in turn.

**Study skills** are dealt with mainly under the heading of **Learning** (Section 6) and the **Study Skills Index** but you need to keep asking yourself the question:

**am I getting the best out of these resources?** Could I make use of them more effectively? This is partly a matter of your own initiative: don't always wait for the teacher or trainer to show you things.

The **informal** learner can get a lot of useful, anecdotal information from **other people**. If they don't know, they often know someone who does. This is true both in professions and in technical, craft or artistic fields. You can also sometimes tap the expertise of **salespeople** in shops, on the back of a transaction: some of these are a real mine of information about their particular product. Others will know less than you do: you'll soon find out.

**Practical manuals** and **self-help books** written for the general public can also be valuable in some fields, and it is worth browsing in libraries and bookshops for them. Increasingly such material is also available in software form.

**WARNING**: if **health and safety** are involved, for example in laboratories or workshops, make sure you receive the proper, official training. **DON'T TAKE RISKS**.

Now note down what action you might take.

## ✉ Resources: what should I do?

# 4 Managing
## organising and coping

**Sixth Form**

| | | | |
|---|---|---|---|
| 4a. All my courses are well designed. | − | ? | + |
| 4b. All my courses are efficiently organised. | − | ? | + |
| 4c. I find the overall workload manageable. | − | ? | + |
| 4d. My studies make reasonable demands on me. | − | ? | + |
| 4e. I manage my studies well. | − | ? | + |

Total

**Further Education**

| | | | |
|---|---|---|---|
| 4a. My course is well designed. | − | ? | + |
| 4b. My course is efficiently run. | − | ? | + |
| 4c. I find the workload manageable. | − | ? | + |
| 4d. The course makes reasonable demands on me. | − | ? | + |
| 4e. I manage my studies well. | − | ? | + |

Total

**Higher Education**

| | | | |
|---|---|---|---|
| 4a. The degree course is well designed. | − | ? | + |
| 4b. The degree course is well run. | − | ? | + |
| 4c. I find the workload manageable. | − | ? | + |
| 4d. The course makes appropriate demands on me. | − | ? | + |
| 4e. I manage my studies well. | − | ? | + |

Total

**Training and Development**

| | | | |
|---|---|---|---|
| 4a. The programme is well designed. | − | ? | + |
| 4b. The programme is efficiently delivered. | − | ? | + |
| 4c. I find the workload manageable. | − | ? | + |
| 4d. The programme makes appropriate demands on me. | − | ? | + |
| 4e. I manage my learning well. | − | ? | + |

Total

**Informal Learning**

| | | | |
|---|---|---|---|
| 4a. I planned my learning project well. | − | ? | + |
| 4b. I organised my learning project efficiently. | − | ? | + |
| 4c. I found the workload manageable. | − | ? | + |
| 4d. The project made reasonable demands on me. | − | ? | + |
| 4e. I coped well with the project. | − | ? | + |

Total

# MANAGING

---

## Key Points

- This whole book is about managing your learning in the broad sense. This particular section is about how your course is designed and organised and how well you cope with it.

- A course should be manageable. That is to say that it should make reasonable or appropriate demands on the people doing it. This is not the same as saying it should be easy.

- There are several reasons why a course may not be manageable. One is that there is simply too much in it. Another problem is that the various parts do not hang together properly. Or there may be a basic lack of clarity about its aims. Does your course suffer from any of these?

- Even if a course is well designed it may be badly run. The documentation may be incomplete or unclear. Information may be incorrect, conflicting or simply late. There may be a lack of communication between the teachers. Messages may get lost. Staff may be unhelpful.

- Poor design and organisation can lead to the course making too few or too many demands, competing pressures, bunching of work and deadlines, venues suddenly changed or sessions cancelled without notice, and a wide range of everyday practical difficulties. Have you experienced any of these things?

✉ **Generally, how well managed is your course? Give it a mark out of ten.**

| /10 |
| --- |

- However, you also need to think about how well you yourself manage the course. In most education and training, managing learning is a shared responsibility, and the learner's share increases the further one goes up the system. Universities typically expect students to manage their learning much more than colleges or schools do, and this can come as a shock in the first year.

- If you cannot cope, is it because you are not organised enough, do not plan ahead, prioritise your work, establish a pattern, and so on? If you can't see how one topic relates to another, is it because you haven't actually tried to relate them? And how deeply have you thought about your own aims?

- Coping also means managing your relationships and your feelings, and some of the difficulties that learners run into stem from these. We cannot isolate our learning from the rest of our lives, but we can try to keep things in proportion and understand how one thing affects another.

- People who are involved in training and development are also usually expected to take some responsibility for managing their own learning, simply because they are responsible adults. So while training design is important, and the organisation of programmes is usually expected to be pretty slick, a lot is down to the participants also.

- In **informal** learning, the whole burden of managing the process falls on the individual (with maybe a little help from his/her friends). The plus side is that the learner is in charge, and can decide about structure, priorities, timing and so on, things which are often beyond the control of the typical student or trainee.

How does any of this affect you?

## ✉ Personal Notes

# Action

A lot depends on the level at which course management decisions are taken.

Some are taken at national level and there is nothing you can do about them. Some are taken at institutional or organisational level, and you may be able to influence these, though **you are more likely to do so as a group than individually**.

Some are taken by individual staff (teachers, lecturers, trainers) and you can often have some impact on these simply through **talking directly to the people concerned**, or using formal mechanisms such as **course evaluation procedures or staff–student committees**.

**Some management decisions are taken by you**. These are the ones you can do most about. For example:

⊠   **Try to prioritise your work into three columns, as follows:**

| MUST DO | SHOULD DO | CAN DO |
| --- | --- | --- |
| | | |
| | | |

Depending on your course, adopt a one-week, two-week or monthly horizon. If you are on a longer course, you may need to work out a plan for each term or semester as well, although plans seem to get less useful the further they stretch into the future.

## Time Management

Work out the average time per week you need to spend on private study outside the taught sessions. Cross-check with your friends to see what the norm is.

If **time** (or lack of it) is a problem, try dividing your study week into **chunks** (two or three hours at a go) and **chinks** (20 or 30 minutes in the middle of other activities). You can use the first for work which needs real concentration and continuity, like writing an essay, and the second for activities such as reading and revising. By putting the two together, you can increase your study hours more than you think, even if you have other commitments related to job or family. The latter will vary through the year and may involve various crises after which you will need to catch up, so build in some leeway.

Look at your natural **rhythm of work**. Do you go in spurts like a sprinter, or at a steady pace, like a long-distance runner? How have you come to work like this? Do you need to change your pattern on this course?

Are you an '**optimiser**' (who wants to do everything as well as possible) or a '**satisficer**' (who does what is appropriate or necessary to get by)?* Note that one is not always better than the other.

**Talk to friends** about personal relationships and emotions if they are worrying you. If the problem becomes persistent or more difficult to cope with, **contact your tutor or a counsellor or go and see your general practitioner (GP)**.

On longer courses, you need consciously to **manage your health**, in terms of diet, fitness, stress and relaxation. Find out about local sports and social facilities. Keep in touch with friends. Give yourself a break. Study can become obsessive and wear you down.

You may find that your **rate of progress** varies, with steep learning curves alternating with 'plateaux' where you seem to get nowhere. Don't worry about this, it is quite normal. If you come up against a block or impasse in one direction, try switching to another for a while. Your mind will continue to work away unconsciously on the first, and when you come back to it, the problem may have sorted itself out.

At a more practical level, if you have a lot of notes and handouts, you will need to develop a good **filing system** so that you don't lose stuff and can find it when you need to. Also, filing will help you to begin organising your thoughts ahead of assignments and exams. Here are some tips:

## 📂 📂 Filing 📂 📂

⇨ Buy several loose-leaf A4 binders, not spiral-bound notebooks. Label them and don't overfill them or it will all fall out. You may need a hole-punch too.

⇨ Use dividers for the main topics. Set up just a few of these at first, and subdivide as you get further into the course. Don't try to be super-organised at the beginning: develop your classification system as you go along.

⇨ Put odd-sized papers or handouts in plastic sleeves so that they don't get lost. If you have bulky booklets, get a box file for them.

⇨ Make a list of contents for each file and also a map of any cross-links between topics. Keep revising and adding to these. Don't worry if they look messy. They will help you to write assignments or revise for exams.

⇨ Write down the complete reference for every source you read. Nothing is more infuriating than trying to track down something which you haven't listed properly.

⇨ Place any assignments/essays/reports at the back of the file, so that you have everything in one place.

You can do most of this on computer too, but you won't usually be able to incorporate handouts into the file.

Now make some notes on what you can do to ensure that your learning is better managed.

# ✉ Managing: what should I do?

# 5 Teaching
## the quality of delivery

**Sixth Form**

| | | |
|---|---|---|
| 5a. All my subjects are well taught. | − ? + |
| 5b. The style of teaching suits the way I learn. | − ? + |
| 5c. I get as much stimulus from the teachers as I need. | − ? + |
| 5d. I get as much support from the teachers as I need. | − ? + |
| 5e. I get on OK with the teachers. | − ? + |

Total

**Further Education**

| | |
|---|---|
| 5a. The teaching on my course is good. | − ? + |
| 5b. The style of teaching suits the way I learn. | − ? + |
| 5c. I get as much stimulus from the lecturers as I need. | − ? + |
| 5d. I get as much support from the lecturers as I need. | − ? + |
| 5e. I get on OK with the lecturers. | − ? + |

Total

**Higher Education**

| | |
|---|---|
| 5a. The teaching on my course is good. | − ? + |
| 5b. The style of teaching suits the way I learn. | − ? + |
| 5c. I get as much stimulus from the lecturers as I need. | − ? + |
| 5d. I get as much support from the lecturers as I need. | − ? + |
| 5e. I have a good working relationship with the lecturers. | − ? + |

Total

**Training and Development**

| | |
|---|---|
| 5a. The training is well delivered. | − ? + |
| 5b. The style of training suits the way I learn. | − ? + |
| 5c. I get as much stimulus from the trainers as I need. | − ? + |
| 5d. I get as much support from the trainers as I need. | − ? + |
| 5e. I have a good rapport with the trainers. | − ? + |

Total

**Informal Learning**

| | |
|---|---|
| 5a. I was good at teaching myself during my learning project. | − ? + |
| 5b. I developed a style of self-teaching that worked for me. | − ? + |
| 5c. I knew how to keep up my interest in the topic. | − ? + |
| 5d. I was able to keep going through the difficult patches. | − ? + |
| 5e. I felt comfortable teaching myself in this way. | − ? + |

Total

# TEACHING

## Key Points

- It is not enough to have the necessary resources organised in a manageable framework: it all has to be properly delivered as well. 'Teaching' in this section covers all forms of teaching, lecturing, tutoring, training, instructing and facilitating, so you should relate what is said to your own particular situation.

- Good teaching/training involves certain skills. Teachers and trainers need to be competent at employing the various methods they use: giving lectures, running classes, managing discussions, handling question and answer, organising practical sessions. Are they?

- However, good teaching/training goes beyond general skills. It has to be geared to the needs of the particular situation: the type of course, the subject, the level, the group and you as an individual. Is the teaching/ training fine-tuned in this way? Do you personally like the style and approach or would you prefer it to be different? If so, how?

- What we think of our teachers and how well we learn from them is not quite the same thing. In fact the relationship between the characteristics of teachers and the process of learning is quite complex, partly because it involves our characteristics and expectations as well.

✉  **What are your teachers/trainers like? Put their initials beside any of the following words which apply to them, and add some more of your own in the spaces. But at the same time ask yourself what you want from them and why.**

| | | |
|---|---|---|
| approachable | disorganised | always in a hurry |
| boring | interesting | knows his/her stuff |
| strict | creative | rigid |
| works you hard | expert | doesn't work you hard |
| | unfair | remote |
| | listens | organised |
| | fair | easy-going |
| good communicator | | poor communicator |
| in touch | inspiring | out of touch |
| has time for you | unclear | doesn't listen |
| clear | enthusiastic | doesn't know his/her stuff |
| in control | not in control | bored |

- Do different people in your group want different things from the teachers/trainers? Do you yourself want different things at different times? Has what you want changed over time, for example during the last year?

- And what about your relationship with your teachers/trainers? We don't always have to like them; we can learn from people we don't particularly get on with, by separating the process from the person. But a really bad relationship can get in the way, at both ends, if only because it diverts both sides from the business of learning. In your case, does anything get in the way?

- Do you communicate with some teachers/trainers better than others? Do you feel on the same wavelength as them? Any idea why?

- What do your teachers/trainers do for you that you couldn't do without them? If all your teachers/trainers were suddenly exiled to some desert island, how would you miss them? Would you miss them?

- **Informal** learning means teaching yourself, except where you can get a bit of help. But even on face-to-face courses, you may have to take over some of the roles and responsibilities of the teacher/trainer. How far do you do this?

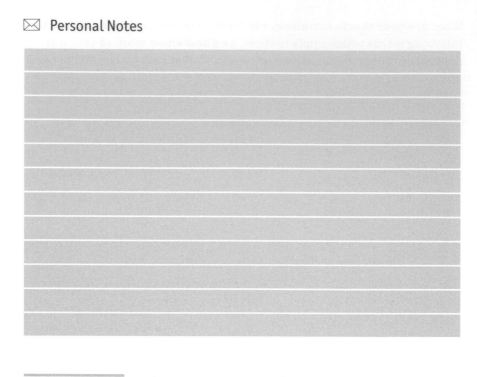

✉ Personal Notes

----

## Action

It is important to think through what you mean by good teaching/training, and it is easier to do this in terms of actual people.

✉ **List three people** who have taught or trained you. For each one, note down what you thought was good about their teaching/training, and what was poor. Try to see what common positive or negative factors there are. Have they to do with the subject-matter? The way the teachers/trainers organised their sessions? Style and delivery? Energy levels? Relationships? Them as people?

| TEACHER/TRAINER | POSITIVE | NEGATIVE |
|---|---|---|
| 1 | | |
| 2 | | |
| 3 | | |

If you are bothered by some aspect of the way you are being taught or trained, the first thing is to **talk it over with other people in the group**, to see if it is just you, or whether they feel the same. If it is a shared concern, you then need to think whether it is something the teacher/trainer could change, or could not. For example, it would not be difficult to give out handouts a bit earlier, or to write up unfamiliar words on the board, and you could ask them (tactfully) to do this.

On the other hand, if people have a rather formal and impersonal style of teaching, they are not likely to change their whole personality. We have to accept that teachers and trainers (like learners) differ and **work with them, not against them**.

Some **informal contact** between teachers and learners can help both sides to remember that they are real people, not just two-dimensional cardboard cut-out roles. For example, field trips or organised excursions can have this effect. However, in the education system such contact depends on the rules and norms of the institution, and may be limited in order to protect the learners. Informal contact in a training environment is usually easier, though it may be influenced by one's place in the organisation.

In further and higher education, students comment on teaching through **evaluation forms** or what are called in training '**happiness sheets**'. These are useful in providing feedback from a whole group, but they can be a bit threatening to the receiver. The same rules apply as when staff comment on students' work: be specific, supportive and constructive. Don't leave him or her with no way out.

The quality of the teaching may influence your choice of subjects, units or modules. Sometimes people go on to study a field at a more advanced level because they were **inspired by a particular teacher or trainer**. Think carefully about how important this personal element is. Would you still want to study that topic with a different teacher/trainer?

If you learn **informally**, you will have absorbed and taken on board yourself most of what teachers/trainers do. Do you still need **external help** with anything? Advice on planning? Locating and vetting materials? Explaining particular problems? Feedback? Support? It is useful to think through to what extent you can do all this yourself, and how far you rely on outside assistance. That will enable you to make better use of the latter.

✉ Teaching: what should I do?

# 6 Learning
the way you learn

**Sixth Form**

6a. I work effectively in class.     − ? +
6b. I work effectively on my own.     − ? +
6c. I have developed good study skills.     − ? +
6d. I can cope equally well with each subject.     − ? +
6e. I have no particular learning problems on my course.     − ? +

Total

**Further Education**

6a. I work effectively in class.     − ? +
6b. I work effectively on my own.     − ? +
6c. I have developed good study skills.     − ? +
6d. I can cope equally well with each part of the course.     − ? +
6e. I have no particular learning problems on this course.     − ? +

Total

**Higher Education**

6a. I work effectively in the taught sessions.     − ? +
6b. I work effectively on my own.     − ? +
6c. I have developed good study skills.     − ? +
6d. I can cope equally well with each part of my degree course.     − ? +
6e. I have no particular learning problems on the course.     − ? +

Total

**Training and Development**

6a. I work effectively in the training sessions.     − ? +
6b. I work effectively on my own.     − ? +
6c. I have developed good learning skills.     − ? +
6d. I can cope equally well with each part of the programme.     − ? +
6e. I have no particular learning problems on this programme.     − ? +

Total

**Informal Learning**

6a. I worked effectively on my own during my project.     − ? +
6b. I developed effective learning skills.     − ? +
6c. I knew how to organise my own learning.     − ? +
6d. I coped equally well with each stage of my project.     − ? +
6e. I had no particular learning problems on my project.     − ? +

Total

# LEARNING

## Key Points

- The previous section was **Teaching**; this one is the other side of the coin, **Learning**.* The whole book is about learning, but this section focuses on your experience of it in your current course or programme.

- Some learning is public, i.e. what we do in a taught class or group. Some is private, i.e. homework, preparation, work on assignments. Are you equally happy with each in your case?

- Learning is partly a matter of skills. If someone is giving a talk or a lecture, you need to be able to take notes. If you are given a book to read, you need to know how to tackle it. Likewise, you need to know how to plan an essay or a report. Organising your information is another important skill. And there are social skills involved in interacting in a group. Have you developed the necessary learning skills, or do you think you lack some?

- Different subjects or topics throw up different learning problems. Are you aware of approaching different parts of your course in different ways? And are you equally comfortable in each case? Do you think you have the right approach for each subject or topic, or do you find some more difficult to tackle than others?

✉ **List three key pieces of advice you would give to a newcomer on your course.**

| |
|---|
| 1 |
| 2 |
| 3 |

- Ask yourself two questions: first, does the way I learn seem to differ from the way my friends/colleagues do, and second, has the way I learn changed over (say) the last two years? Each of these may throw light on your current approach.

- Do you feel more comfortable with some kinds of teaching/training methods than others? For example, do you prefer more or less structured sessions, more or less formality? Do you prefer one-to-one, small group, or large group sessions? Do you get more out of discussion or practical, hands-on classes? If so, why? Has your previous experience something to do with this?

- You may think that you have particular study problems. For example, some people complain that they can't concentrate, others that their memory is poor. Such problems do exist, though they may in fact point to deeper issues such as a lack of interest or real understanding; we can usually concentrate on things which are important to us, and we usually remember things that make sense to us. Are your study problems the real problems?

- Learning is not always a positive experience. It involves making mistakes, and is often a process of trial and error. And sometimes it can feel like you are going backwards, or round in circles. All this is quite normal. It's not just you.

Note down any thoughts about your own learning below.

## ✉ Personal Notes

# Action

People sometimes say that the most important thing in a marriage is to **talk**. The same is true of learning. The problem is that we are so busy learning X, Y or Z that there is no time to talk about the experience of learning it. Teachers and trainers feel under pressure to cover the syllabus, students and trainees are worrying about assignments and the whole public system of assessment reinforces these priorities. Learning becomes a hidden, almost secret activity.

Try **chatting** to your friends, peers or colleagues about the way you learn and any problems you have. You won't want to bore them, but you will probably find that they share many of the same experiences, and that you are by no means as different or unusual as you might think.

Try keeping a personal **learning diary**, which records your experience and problems over a period of months. If you fill this in say twice a week, you should have plenty to look back on at the end of the period. Such a diary can help you to reflect more systematically on what you are doing, and build up your own 'learning biography'.

> _Friday, 22nd Feb_
>
> _Rotten cold all week and feeling a bit low. I suppose it's the time of year. And the work seems to be piling up again, three essays and the project. With this modular system the pressure is on all the time. Didn't get as much done over Christmas as planned but then none of my friends did either. Easter will be catch-up time. But getting really into the social history stuff now, got a good lecturer this term. He puts it across really well. Maybe I will go on with it next year._

If you are worried about particular learning skills (such as reading and writing, communication, planning, time management, information retrieval) you may be able to attend **workshops** which deal with them.

Learning problems stemming from a lack of basic knowledge of **maths, computing or languages** are dealt with in **Foundations** (Section 14). See also **Tips for the Terrified**.

Above all, get as much **feedback** on your work as possible, as frequently as possible. Don't just find out the mark or grade: find out why. You can then begin to see how your approach led to the results that it did.

✉  Learning: what should I do?

# PART B: INFLUENCES

The way you learn is influenced by a wide range of factors. Some of these, such as your own motivation and self-belief, have to do with you, although they often reflect what has happened to you in the past. Others relate to the kind of environment you are learning in, and the people involved. It is important to explore these factors, and how they affect not just your thinking but also your feelings.

When you have finished **Motivation** (Section 13), look back at some of the sections in Part B where you scored +3 or more, making any notes you want. These will help to give you a more rounded view of your learning.

# 7 Modelling
## learning by example

**Sixth Form**

| | | | |
|---|---|---|---|
| 7a. My teachers are important to me. | − | ? | + |
| 7b. I learn a lot from the example of my teachers. | − | ? | + |
| 7c. My teachers put across their subjects well. | − | ? | + |
| 7d. My teachers make their subjects come alive. | − | ? | + |
| 7e. I respect my teachers. | − | ? | + |

Total

**Further Education**

| | | | |
|---|---|---|---|
| 7a. My lecturers are important to me. | − | ? | + |
| 7b. I learn a lot from the example of my lecturers. | − | ? | + |
| 7c. My lecturers put across their subjects well. | − | ? | + |
| 7d. My lecturers make their subjects come alive. | − | ? | + |
| 7e. I respect the expertise of my lecturers. | − | ? | + |

Total

**Higher Education**

| | | | |
|---|---|---|---|
| 7a. My lecturers are important to me. | − | ? | + |
| 7b. I learn a lot from the example of my lecturers. | − | ? | + |
| 7c. My lecturers present their subjects well. | − | ? | + |
| 7d. My lecturers are good models in their own field. | − | ? | + |
| 7e. My lecturers have made a deep impression on me. | − | ? | + |

Total

**Training and Development**

| | | | |
|---|---|---|---|
| 7a. My trainers are important to me. | − | ? | + |
| 7b. I learn a lot from the example of my trainers. | − | ? | + |
| 7c. I respect the expertise of my trainers. | − | ? | + |
| 7d. My trainers practise what they preach. | − | ? | + |
| 7e. My trainers have made a strong impression on me. | − | ? | + |

Total

**Informal Learning**

| | | | |
|---|---|---|---|
| 7a. Other people were important in my learning project. | − | ? | + |
| 7b. I learned a lot from the example of other people. | − | ? | + |
| 7c. Other people acted as models for me in my project. | − | ? | + |
| 7d. Other people showed me the way in my project. | − | ? | + |
| 7e. Other people meant a lot to me in my project. | − | ? | + |

Total

# MODELLING

---

## Key Points

- Modelling means learning from the behaviour or example of other people.\* Parents, older brothers or sisters, friends, sportsmen and women, pop stars, historical figures can all act as models whom we try to be like. Modelling is also important in the workplace, when we learn from the example of more experienced colleagues.

- Not all models are teachers/trainers and not all teachers/trainers are models. But most teachers/trainers make some impression and have some influence on those they teach or train, even if neither side is always conscious of this. And modelling is particularly important where we are learning some kind of occupation or process.

- This means that modelling is central to vocational courses (e.g. becoming a mechanic or a cook or a secretary) and professional courses (e.g. becoming a designer or doctor or lawyer). This is because we are learning not only to do but also to be these things, to perform these roles and act in these ways.

- However, modelling may also be important in academic subjects where we are learning not just the content of (say) economics, history or biology, but also the process: how to approach economic problems, how to think like an historian, how to do science.

- And modelling is a key process in the arts. Many writers, painters and musicians have developed through modelling themselves on other artists, though usually they then go on to find their own voice or style. A lot of teaching in these fields consists of deliberate or unconscious modelling, as it does also in crafts and sports.

✉ **How important is modelling in your field of study? Ring your response.**

| | | | |
|---|---|---|---|
| not important | quite important | important | very important |

> 📖  If it is not important at all, you may want to stop here and move on to the next section. But are you quite sure?

- You may not be aware that you are treating other people as models, or that they are treating you as one. But think about it. How have you come to be as you are? Why do you talk, dress, behave the way you do? Could your friends spot the influences on you? Models may be people we know or simply know of. The essential point is that we look up to them and try to be like them in some way.

- Learning which involves modelling can be a very powerful process, affecting not just our conscious thinking but also our unconscious values and preferences. It is not entirely rational or under our control. Think of the influence of charismatic political leaders, for good or ill. Nor is modelling always a positive process in learning. There may be negative models whom we try to avoid being like. Even with positive models, there is a risk that they may stifle our own personality.

- It may not matter too much if you don't regard your teachers/trainers as models, though it will usually strengthen your learning if you do. But if you see them as negative models, or think that there is a tension between what they say and what they do, that can set up a worrying contradiction. And different teachers may model contrasting approaches.

- The people you work or study with may also be positive or negative models for you. And you may be a model for them. Peer influence is particularly strong in the teenage years.

- In training and development, it is important to ask who the real models are. Is it the trainers? Or the on-the-job practitioners? Is there any conflict between the two? Is there a gap between theory and practice? Is gender an aspect of modelling for you, in relation to jobs or in other ways?

- People who learn **informally** are often quite independent-minded and may not need anyone to imitate or emulate. But they may still make use of other people as models for learning particular kinds of skill or behaviour: they can choose to be influenced in this way.

Note down your own thoughts on modelling.

✉ Personal notes

_____

## Action

If you want to explore modelling and understand its place in your learning, you can start by making **a list of the five or six most significant figures** in your life, beginning with your childhood, and then working on through adolescence and into adulthood: a kind of informal autobiography. Are there any teachers or trainers among them? If there are, what did they represent for you? How did they influence you?

Think also about your **current course**. Is there anyone you would single out as a model, teacher/trainer or other learner? Again, what do they represent for you? What do they embody?

On the other hand, modelling may concern you in various ways. You may feel that you are under too strong an influence, and are in danger of **losing your own identity**. This is a particular risk in subjects which are emotionally charged, such as art or drama, or where you are working closely with a much more experienced or prestigious person in a professional field such as law or medicine. If there are other people going through the same experience, **talk it over with them**, though sometimes it is better to do this with someone who is totally outside the situation and can therefore see it more objectively.

Another way of exploring this is to use two scales (see box) with '**self-directed**' at one end and '**other-directed**' at the other.* The first means relying on your own image and judgement of yourself, the second on other people's images and judgements. Get a friend to place you somewhere on the first spectrum (not necessarily at either end) and place himself/herself on the second. Do the same yourself independently. Then compare your perceptions. What does this tell you about yourselves? Repeat with another person if you can.

| **You** | Self-directed | x | x | x | x | x | Other-directed |
| **Me** | Self-directed | x | x | x | x | x | Other-directed |

Modelling is a personal process, and it really needs to be talked through on a personal level. Ideally, it is best explored with a small number of other people whom you trust and can talk openly to. That probably means your **peers or friends**, although a sensitive teacher or trainer should be aware of this aspect of his or her work.

This may be an aspect of your learning where there are no simple or concrete actions to take, but note down any ways in which you would like the situation to change.

## ✉ Modelling: what should I do?

# 8 Support
## getting help

**Sixth Form**

| | | | |
|---|---|---|---|
| 8a. My teachers are approachable. | − | ? | + |
| 8b. I can discuss most problems I have with my teachers. | − | ? | + |
| 8c. I can get support from my friends if I need it. | − | ? | + |
| 8d. I get support from my family if I need it. | − | ? | + |
| 8e. If I want help or advice, there is someone I can turn to. | − | ? | + |

Total

**Further Education**

| | | | |
|---|---|---|---|
| 8a. My lecturers are approachable. | − | ? | + |
| 8b. I can discuss most problems I have with my lecturers. | − | ? | + |
| 8c. I can get support from my friends if I need it. | − | ? | + |
| 8d. I get support from my family if I need it. | − | ? | + |
| 8e. If I want help or advice, there is someone I can turn to. | − | ? | + |

Total

**Higher Education**

| | | | |
|---|---|---|---|
| 8a. My lecturers are approachable. | − | ? | + |
| 8b. I can discuss most problems I have with my lecturers. | − | ? | + |
| 8c. I can get support from my friends if I need it. | − | ? | + |
| 8d. I get support from my family if I need it. | − | ? | + |
| 8e. If I want help or advice, there is someone I can turn to. | − | ? | + |

Total

**Training and Development**

| | | | |
|---|---|---|---|
| 8a. The trainers are approachable. | − | ? | + |
| 8b. I can share most problems I have with the trainers. | − | ? | + |
| 8c. I get support from the other participants if I need it. | − | ? | + |
| 8d. I get support from people in my job if I need it. | − | ? | + |
| 8e. If I want help or advice, there is someone I can turn to. | − | ? | + |

Total

**Informal Learning**

| | | | |
|---|---|---|---|
| 8a. I found people approachable in my learning project. | − | ? | + |
| 8b. There were people I could turn to when I had problems. | − | ? | + |
| 8c. I got as much support from others as I needed. | − | ? | + |
| 8d. I got support from the people around me. | − | ? | + |
| 8e. If I wanted help or advice, there was someone I could turn to. | − | ? | + |

Total

# SUPPORT

## Key Points

- We all run into problems when we learn. Some of these have to do with the learning process itself: the content or subject-matter. But there may be other kinds of problems as well that affect the way we learn, to do with ourselves, our relationships and the situation we are in.

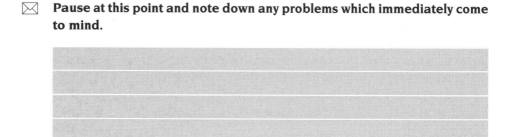 **Pause at this point and note down any problems which immediately come to mind.**

- If you do run into problems, can you get help? Whom do you turn to for advice with learning problems? Staff? Friends? Family? Colleagues? Others? And if you have wider problems, whom can you go to for help and support?

- Are there some teachers/trainers whom people typically turn to? Are there any central services which offer study support? Is professional guidance or counselling available if needed? How would you feel about approaching such services?

- The people closest to us are not always the best at supporting us. They may simply be too close. Or they may have their own agenda.

- You may be quite self-reliant and tend to sort out problems or worries yourself. If you are an **informal** learner you may have to be. But even then it is worth thinking about whom you do or do not get support from.

- On the negative side, is there anyone who actually undermines your learning? Who is the opposite of supportive and helpful? Do such people have much effect on you? How do you cope with this?

- Problems sometimes arise at particular stages in a course or particular times of year. For example, they can come in the early stages when you are trying to settle in, or after Christmas when people are generally feeling low, in the run-up to exams, or even after the whole thing is over (withdrawal symptoms). Are you aware of any pattern in your case? When do you feel under greatest stress? When do you most need support?

- In the training and development field, a sudden change of role can create problems. For example, when an experienced or senior person becomes a 'learner' again, it can be quite difficult to adapt to the loss of authority and control. Losing one's job or retiring involve major changes of role and relationships. Have you experienced any such role losses/reversals/ conflicts?

- The phrase 'emotional intelligence' is sometimes used to describe the way we manage and express our feelings.* Do you think you have changed in this respect over recent years? Are you better able to live with your emotions than you were? And can you support others in this way?

✉  Personal Notes

# Action

Writing things down sometimes helps. **List the main problems you think you face**. Leave the list for a day or two, and add to it if anything else occurs to you. Then either go through it yourself or with someone else whom you trust, and see what you might do about each one.

Some people prefer a more structured approach as follows. Divide the problems into four types, in terms of whether they are **intellectual** (to do with knowledge, understanding, skill, etc.) or **emotional** (motivation, confidence, relationships, etc.) and **short term** (the next few weeks) or **long term** (months or years). Don't get hung up on classifying them, they may well overlap. Think about how you could address each one: you may need to tackle different kinds of problems in different ways.

|  | SHORT TERM | LONG TERM |
|---|---|---|
| **INTELLECTUAL** | | |
| **EMOTIONAL** | | |

If you have a **personal tutor or adviser**, go to see him or her. That is what such people are for. Sometimes they are more helpful than you expect when you actually ask them; they may not have been aware that you had a problem at all. It could be useful to send them a brief note beforehand to give them time to think about it. You should always let staff know of any **health problems** which might affect your work.

If your tutor/supervisor is not the listening kind, go to **a member of staff you know** already through everyday work. On the whole, teachers and trainers take this pastoral side of their work conscientiously. If you feel that the problem is a more persistent or serious one, you should think about getting **professional help from a support service or through your GP**. Friends/family/colleagues are not always best equipped to cope with such issues.

In a training context, concrete problems should be dealt with through a **line manager** and may for example come up in appraisal sessions. However **colleagues**, especially more experienced ones, may also be a useful resource in terms of more personal issues which you may not want to share with the organisation. Is there someone whom you can turn to as a formal or informal **mentor**?

Counsellors talk about people '**presenting**' with an initial problem behind which there lies a deeper problem, which emerges later in the consultation, and which the person finds more difficult to identify or express. Can you relate to this?

If you are a self-directed **informal** learner, by definition you will have to be more **self-reliant**. However, it is still useful to think about what sources of support you have or can draw on if need be. Even thinking aloud to others can elicit useful suggestions.

## ✉ Support: what should I do?

# 9 Interaction
## learning with others

**Sixth Form**

9a.  I get on well with the others in my classes.                             −  ?  +
9b.  I enjoy working with the others in my classes.                           −  ?  +
9c.  I learn a lot from working with the others.                              −  ?  +
9d.  Group interaction is an important part of my learning.                   −  ?  +
9e.  The groups I am in work well together.                                   −  ?  +

Total

**Further Education**

9a.  I get on well with the others in my classes.                             −  ?  +
9b.  I enjoy working with the others in my classes.                           −  ?  +
9c.  I learn a lot from working with the others.                              −  ?  +
9d.  Group work is an important part of my learning.                          −  ?  +
9e.  The groups I am in work well together.                                   −  ?  +

Total

**Higher Education**

9a.  I get on well with the others doing my course.                           −  ?  +
9b.  I enjoy working with the others doing my course.                         −  ?  +
9c.  I learn a lot from the others on my course.                              −  ?  +
9d.  Group interaction is an important part of my learning.                   −  ?  +
9e.  The groups I am in work well together.                                   −  ?  +

Total

**Training and Development**

9a.  I get on well with the other participants on the programme.              −  ?  +
9b.  I enjoy working with the other participants.                             −  ?  +
9c.  I get a lot from working with the other participants.                    −  ?  +
9d.  Group interaction is an important part of the programme.                 −  ?  +
9e.  The groups I am in work well together.                                   −  ?  +

Total

**Informal Learning**

9a.  My learning project involved working with others.                        −  ?  +
9b.  I enjoyed working with others.                                           −  ?  +
9c.  I gained a lot from working with others.                                 −  ?  +
9d.  I could not have learned what I did entirely on my own.                  −  ?  +
9e.  I worked well with others.                                               −  ?  +

Total

# INTERACTION

## Key points

- A lot of learning is an individual business. For example, if you are learning to type or use a computer it doesn't matter much whether you are doing it on your own or in a group. The same is true of most skills: you have to practise them until you have mastered them, and no one else can do it for you. Learning factual information is also largely a solo affair, and our understanding of ideas and concepts is ultimately a personal thing, something we have to make our own.

- However, most of the learning we do benefits from some element of group interaction. Why? There are various reasons:

  ⇨ Groups can gather more information than individuals

  ⇨ Groups can divide up tasks and share the work

  ⇨ Groups can provide mutual stimulus and challenge

  ⇨ Groups can offer support to their members

  ⇨ Groups can contribute different angles on the same problem or topic

  ⇨ Groups force us to explain what we mean

  ⇨ Groups give us feedback.

- In education and training, we sometimes remember the group when we have forgotten much else. Indeed, a good group can sometimes compensate for poor teaching, and create a bond among its members in coping with it. However, groups do not always work well. A lot depends on the 'chemistry' and the personalities involved. And the interaction can vary from one meeting to the next, for no apparent reason.

- Large groups may work less well than small groups. Groups can be unfair and turn nasty. Existing groups may exclude newcomers or marginalise people who are different in some way. Some groups can be wholly dysfunctional.

Others are merely a waste of time. But the learning potential of groups is great, simply because learning is so often a shared thing.

- How important is working with others to you? Do you gain much from it, or would you prefer to be mainly on your own? Some people like to work individually, so that they are more in control of their own subject-matter, can focus on their own priorities and go at their own pace. There is nothing wrong in that; it is simply a matter of learning style.

**What about you? To what extent do you like working in a group or on your own? Ring your preference. (Or does it depend . . . ?)**

| in a group | X | X | X | X | X | on my own |

- Not all interaction need be in large groups. For example you might take part in 'peer-learning' (usually pairs or threes) or 'cooperative learning' (typically groups of about five). These are meant to provide the benefits of interaction without some of the baggage of group dynamics. Have you experienced these modes of learning? If so, how useful have you found them?

- If you are engaged in **informal** learning, do you work mainly on your own? If so, do you miss the buzz of a group, or are you happy to get on with things by yourself? A lot of **informal** learning goes on in little networks or clusters, brought together by a shared interest or problem. This is particularly true of workplace learning, where people tackle a problem together, and learning related to hobbies and leisure activities.

Do you like group work? How important is it to you? Describe your own experience overleaf.

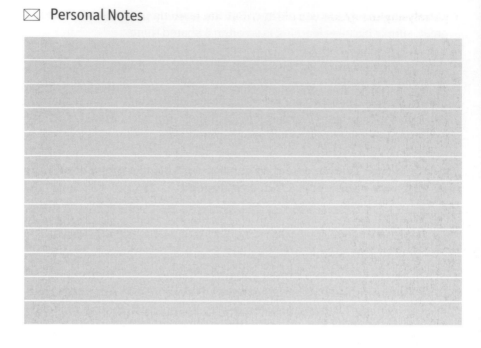

✉ Personal Notes

---

## Action

If you work mainly on your own, think about whether you are **providing for yourself** some of the things you would get from a group – the challenge, the different perspectives, the criticism, the momentum, the support.

**Don't worry** if the group you are in doesn't jell immediately. It can take time for people to get used to one another, although teachers and trainers nowadays often begin with some 'ice-breakers' (which may or may not work). It is normal for people to want to 'test the water' especially if they are new to this kind of experience.

Try **analysing the group** you are in. There are three things to look for:

---

## Group Interaction

⇨ **Who talks to whom?** Are there any patterns? Regular duets or trios? Any 'stars' or 'isolates'? Does seating affect this? Where do you sit? Whom do you talk to? For example people often talk across a group rather than to one side, though sometimes you get little private conversations going on. Body language can also tell you a good deal about communication.

⇨ **What roles do people play?** Leader? Challenger? Devil's advocate (who likes stirring things up)? Diplomat? Timekeeper? Agenda-minder? Joker? Spectator? What role or roles do you play? Are there any you avoid? A mixture of roles is needed for a group to function well. People often worry about the level of conflict in groups, but they can become too cosy also.

⇨ **What phases does the group go through?** How does it begin? How does it finish? And what happens in between? Any false starts or premature conclusions? Does it go along in a straight line or off on tangents or round in circles? Are there distinct stages in the process? And how are the conclusions or decisions reached, if they are?

---

Group work can seem easy. All you apparently have to do is sit there and talk. But unless people have done the **preparatory work**, they may not have much to say. Do you? Do others?

Each time you finish a group session, ask yourself two questions: first, did the group **complete its task**, and second, did the group **interact well?** The answer may be yes to one rather than both: sometimes you can have a good time and get nowhere or an awful time and get things done.

**If your group is not working well**, discuss it with a few other people to see what they think. Not all teachers/trainers are naturally good at managing groups and you may be able to help the dynamics along, perhaps by identifying and playing a **missing role**. You can't expect the teacher to do all the work.

Your interactive learning may be with one or two other people rather than a whole group, and this makes it even more personal. People work together in pairs because they both get something out of it. What do each of you bring to the partnership? What kind of '**invisible handshake**' is there between you? Try reflecting on that, especially if things seem to be going wrong.

If you learn **informally**, think about any small groups or associations you belong to. What do you get from them? And what do you give to them? **Informal** doesn't necessarily mean individual, and a lot of exchange can go on among people interested in the same things.

Note down what you might do to improve this aspect of your learning.

## ✉ Interaction: what should I do?

# 10 Environment
## the learning setting

**Sixth Form**

10a. My school/college provides a good environment for learning.    − ? +
10b. There is a good learning environment in my classes.    − ? +
10c. We can get on with our work in class without disruption.    − ? +
10d. I can get on with my own work when I want to.    − ? +
10e. I have no problems with my learning environment.    − ? +

Total

**Further Education**

10a. The college provides a good environment for learning.    − ? +
10b. There is a good learning environment on my course.    − ? +
10c. We can get on with our work in class without disruption.    − ? +
10d. I can get on with my own work when I want to.    − ? +
10e. I have no problems with my learning environment.    − ? +

Total

**Higher Education**

10a. The university provides a good environment for learning.    − ? +
10b. My department creates a good environment for learning.    − ? +
10c. There is a good learning environment on my course.    − ? +
10d. I can get on with my own work when I need to.    − ? +
10e. I have no problems with my learning environment.    − ? +

Total

**Training and Development**

10a. The training programme provides a good learning environment.    − ? +
10b. There is a good learning environment in the training sessions.    − ? +
10c. I can get on with my learning when I need to.    − ? +
10d. I have no problems with my learning environment.    − ? +
10e. I would describe my learning environment as positive.    − ? +

Total

**Informal Learning**

10a. I managed to create a good learning environment for myself.    − ? +
10b. My environment helped rather than hindered me.    − ? +
10c. I had enough time to get on with my project.    − ? +
10d. I had places where I could get on with my project.    − ? +
10e. I had no problems with my learning environment.    − ? +

Total

# ENVIRONMENT

## Key Points

- The word environment simply means what is around us or what we are surrounded by. Here it is being used to mean what is around you when you learn.

- This is partly a physical matter: the campus, site or venue, and within that the buildings, rooms and spaces you work in. Your physical environment may affect your learning directly, if your work depends on having certain facilities, although a lot of these have been covered under the heading of **Resources** (Section 3). But if you need to work regularly in a studio, lab or workshop, the quality of the physical environment will be crucial.

- Your physical environment may also affect you indirectly, for example in terms of the layout of a classroom, how it is arranged, where people sit, and so on. And the physical environment can affect us emotionally as well, depending on whether it is pleasant, stimulating, drab or uncomfortable. The physical environment may also send out social signals: the annex may not be quite on a par with the main college. If you study mainly at home or at your place of work you need to consider those environments too and how they help or hinder your learning.

✉ **Pause here and note down any effects your physical environment has on the way you learn.**

- However, it is the social environment which is likely to have the greatest effect on your learning. We can often remember the ethos or atmosphere of a course or class long afterwards. How would you describe your social learning environment? Welcoming or offputting? Formal or relaxed? Supportive or threatening? Dull or exciting?

- At worst, environment can get in the way of learning. If there are many discipline problems in class, teachers have to spend their time managing these rather than actually teaching. Likewise, you might find it difficult to work at home for various reasons. By contrast, a good atmosphere in class, at home or in the workplace can make learning easier and much more pleasant.

- If you are living with other students in halls or flats, this may affect your studies. Most undergraduates enjoy the independence and social life, but can you get on with your work? Are there too many distractions? Who does the washing up? Living together like this is itself a form of learning.

- One problem in the training sector is that there may be a gap or even conflict between the training environment and the real work environment. One may contrast with the other, and even seem as if it is on a different planet. How do you reconcile the two?

- Another way to think about your learning environment is in terms of cultures.* What kind of little tribe or subculture is your school, college or department? What binds it together? What are the ground-rules or shared values? What jokes do people tell? How do they dress? Do you feel you belong?

- If you study part-time or at a distance, how does this affect your learning? Positively or negatively? Do you think that you have the same quality of environment as full-time students?

- Residential study is meant to have advantages in terms of creating a real 'learning community'. If you are attending such a course or workshop, how does it seem to you? Is there a strong, collegial feeling? Or do you find it restrictive or intrusive?

✉ Personal Notes

## Action

Short of leaving and moving somewhere else, it may be difficult to make any major changes. After all, we are talking about the whole structure and ethos of a place, and it usually takes more than one person to alter that, particularly if it is well established. However, there are some **practical measures you can take**.

If you don't like the physical environment, see if there are any small changes which can be made to improve it, and suggest these to those in charge. Staff may not fully realise how you experience the environment as a student or trainee. **Minor alterations in timetabling, layout or other practical arrangements** can sometimes make a surprising difference.

If you don't like the general environment, try to create a **micro-environment** of your own with some of your friends. You are unlikely to be the only person who feels as you do, and you may be able to survive quite happily as a little group, supporting one another.

You may be able to compensate by **spending more time in one part of your environment than another**. People often choose to work in some places rather than others. If life is difficult at home, perhaps you can spend more time at school/college/ university, or vice versa. Even at college or university, you can spend more time in one part than another.

At a basic level, try to ensure that your environment doesn't actually stop you learning because of **constant disruption in class**. If it does, then you have a right to **complain**. This goes for any kind of bullying or victimisation as well. If you are not happy in your current student accommodation, you should consider **moving**. If you are easily distracted, try **timetabling** library or laboratory study periods for yourself as if they were normal classes.

If you have experienced **two contrasting learning environments**, for example in different classes or institutions, make a list of the differences between them. This will tell you something not only about them but also your reaction to them. Discuss this with others if you can.

## Getting in the Mood

If you study a lot at home, try to create a **dedicated study space** for yourself: somewhere that you associate with working and which gets you in the mood. The choice is up to you. Some people like the kitchen because tea and coffee are at hand, others find too many reminders of chores to be done. Some people need the quiet of a bedroom which is out of the way. Others prefer a bit of background music (which they like but not too much) and activity because it is more normal. Make sure you have good lighting, seating, heating and ventilation. A cold room, poor illumination and bad posture all create strain, which you may not notice when you are concentrating.

Getting yourself in the mood is also a matter of **timing**. If you have had a busy day doing other things (job, looking after children, etc.) try going into neutral for half an hour (read the paper, have a chat) to let your mind settle before you begin. If you worry about forgetting things you need to do the next day, keep a list to hand where you can note them down: that will relieve the anxiety. Some people develop little rituals before they start work (arranging the pens, walking up and down, changing into something different, etc.). These are quite natural but beware that they don't simply become delaying actions (*just another cup of coffee/one more phone call and then . . .*): sooner or later you have to get down to it.

Now make a note of any ways you think you could improve your learning environment.

## ✉ Environment: what should I do?

# 11  Context
## wider influences

**Sixth Form**

| | | | | |
|---|---|---|---|---|
| 11a. | My family takes my education seriously. | − | ? | + |
| 11b. | My friends take education seriously. | − | ? | + |
| 11c. | The community I live in takes education seriously. | − | ? | + |
| 11d. | The people around me take an interest in my education. | − | ? | + |
| 11e. | Nobody discourages me from studying. | − | ? | + |

Total

**Further Education**

| | | | | |
|---|---|---|---|---|
| 11a. | My family takes my education seriously. | − | ? | + |
| 11b. | My friends take education seriously. | − | ? | + |
| 11c. | The community I live in takes education seriously. | − | ? | + |
| 11d. | The people around me take an interest in my education. | − | ? | + |
| 11e. | Nobody discourages me from studying. | − | ? | + |

Total

**Higher Education**

| | | | | |
|---|---|---|---|---|
| 11a. | My family takes my education seriously. | − | ? | + |
| 11b. | My friends take education seriously. | − | ? | + |
| 11c. | Higher education is valued in the community I come from. | − | ? | + |
| 11d. | The people close to me take an interest in my studies. | − | ? | + |
| 11e. | The people close to me encourage me to get my degree. | − | ? | + |

Total

**Training and Development**

| | | | | |
|---|---|---|---|---|
| 11a. | Training and development are important in my job. | − | ? | + |
| 11b. | My organisation takes training seriously. | − | ? | + |
| 11c. | The people I work with take training seriously. | − | ? | + |
| 11d. | My superiors take an interest in my development. | − | ? | + |
| 11e. | The people around me encourage me to go on learning. | − | ? | + |

Total

**Informal Learning**

| | | | | |
|---|---|---|---|---|
| 11a. | Those who are close to me encouraged my learning. | − | ? | + |
| 11b. | The people I know were positive about my learning project. | − | ? | + |
| 11c. | Informal learning is valued in my community. | − | ? | + |
| 11d. | The people around me took an interest in what I was learning. | − | ? | + |
| 11e. | Nobody discouraged me from learning. | − | ? | + |

Total

# CONTEXT

## Key Points

- Beyond the immediate environment of your course, the wider world affects the way you learn. Your family, partner, friends, colleagues, workplace, community: all of these form the context of your learning.

- Family can have a major influence, especially when you are young. Not just a mother or father, but brothers and sisters, especially older ones, can also shape your attitudes or set an example. And sometimes a person outside the immediate family, such as a grandparent, uncle or aunt, can influence you as well. If you yourself are a parent, your family commitments may well affect your studies, especially in terms of time and availability and the inevitable emergencies (the cat or dog being sick, etc.)

- It makes a difference if you know people who have already done something which you are thinking of doing, such as getting an apprenticeship or going to college. They can show you that it is possible and sometimes give you advice.

- Friends are another important influence. Most people in their teens find it difficult to ignore the pressures of their peers. Those pressures might work for or against education. The other obvious example of peer-group pressure is in the workplace. Most of us want to belong, and get on with the people around us, and that can affect our attitude to education or training. It is difficult to swim against the tide, though some people do.

- The take-up of education and training varies across social classes and communities. If you come from a community or culture where education or training is valued, it makes it easier and more natural to be committed to learning; and the opposite is true. If you come from overseas, you will bring with you some of the educational and training values of your own country.

- If you have a partner, he or she may or may not encourage you to go on with education and training. Sometimes partners feel excluded by this, or fear that they will lose or become estranged from the other person as he or she makes new friends on a different basis.

✉ **Place any of the following in order of importance in terms of their influence on you as a learner: family, friends, job, partner, community, country.**

| 1 | 2 | 3 | 4 | 5 | 6 |
|---|---|---|---|---|---|

- If you move away from your own home and community, for example to go to university, the situation changes. The university may become your new community, even your new home. You can lose touch with old friends, and become distanced from your family. Has this happened at all to you?

- As regards training and development, the influence of your organisation, your boss and your colleagues can be enormous. Opportunities for training are not evenly available to everyone: for example part-timers usually get less training than full-timers, and people in lower grades less than those in higher ones.

- The role or roles you have can also affect your and others' attitudes. For example, in the past, retired people were not expected to go back into education, though this has now changed. Likewise, women in the home often faced resistance to the idea. One of the main barriers is that people come to think 'education or training is not for me'. They absorb and inter-nalise the views and prejudices of others, until such views become part of their own outlook and self-concept.

- Gender may also be a factor which affects you. Some subjects tend to have male or female stereotypes, though this is less true than in the past. Has your gender influenced the way you or others have thought about your education or training choices?

- If you learn **informally** on your own, you may be more independent and less influenced by the people around you. But even then they can support or undermine your learning, often in small ways: a small word of encourage-ment, a passing sarcasm. And there are many **informal networks** of people, who have particular interests, which provide stimulus and support. **Informal** learning is not necessarily a solitary activity; it can form its own little world.

## Informal Networks

Here are some examples of informal networks that commonly exist. Some of them relate to family, some to work and some to social or leisure interests. Do you belong to any of them? If not, can you think of others that you do belong to?

Animal-lovers (all kinds); art; car enthusiasts; chess; clubbing; cookery; community or neighbourhood groups; computing; DIY; fashion; films; fishing; gardening; keep-fit; literature; local history; music (all kinds); parents of pre-school children; parents with children at the same school; people who have (or care for those who have) the same illness; people who work together; people who go to the same pub; photography; political activists; professional associations; ramblers; real ale; religious groups; sports (all kinds); travel clubs; wine lovers; yoga.

✉ **Personal Notes**

## Action

Of all the factors which affect your learning, this is probably the one you can do least about. You are born into a family and a community, and even if you choose your friends, you are surrounded by the people who happen to be there. The same is even truer of the workplace: your organisation and your colleagues are a 'given'. No wonder people sometimes feel trapped.

As with all the other headings, however, **awareness** counts for something. If you can understand your situation better, and analyse the reasons why things are positive or negative, it can at least help you cope with them in your own mind. And you may think of ways out.

For example, if you face resistance or indifference within your immediate family, you may be able to turn to more **distant relations** for help and support. Because they are less involved, they may be able to see things more objectively. Don't be put off by having a particularly successful older brother or sister: **find your own strengths**.

If you are coming under a lot of **peer pressure** to conform, it helps to find something else which will earn you the group's respect, and confirm your membership of it, while allowing you to go your own way in other things.

**If your work environment is negative** in this respect, then perhaps you should think about changing job. It is not just a question of your own career development: any organisation nowadays which does not take training seriously is unlikely to be able to keep up with changes in the marketplace or general economic and social environment.

If you think there is nothing or no one in your immediate context who shares or supports your learning interests, you may have to look further afield for **models** (see Section 7).

✉  Context: what should I do?

# 12  Belief

## confidence and expectations

### Sixth Form

| | | | |
|---|---|---|---|
| 12a. I think I am capable of working at this level. | − | ? | + |
| 12b. I am confident that I can learn what I need to. | − | ? | + |
| 12c. I believe I can succeed on this course. | − | ? | + |
| 12d. I think I can cope with any difficulties I have. | − | ? | + |
| 12e. My teachers believe in me. | − | ? | + |

Total

### Further Education

| | | | |
|---|---|---|---|
| 12a. I think I am capable of working at this level. | − | ? | + |
| 12b. I am confident that I can learn what I need to. | − | ? | + |
| 12c. I believe I can succeed on this course. | − | ? | + |
| 12d. I think I can cope with any problems I have. | − | ? | + |
| 12e. My lecturers believe in me. | − | ? | + |

Total

### Higher Education

| | | | |
|---|---|---|---|
| 12a. I think I am capable of working at degree level. | − | ? | + |
| 12b. I am confident that I can meet the demands of the course. | − | ? | + |
| 12c. I believe I can succeed in getting my degree. | − | ? | + |
| 12d. I think I can cope with any problems I encounter. | − | ? | + |
| 12e. My lecturers have confidence in me. | − | ? | + |

Total

### Training and Development

| | | | |
|---|---|---|---|
| 12a. I believe I am capable of working at this level. | − | ? | + |
| 12b. I think I can meet the challenges of the programme. | − | ? | + |
| 12c. I believe I can achieve the objectives of my training. | − | ? | + |
| 12d. I am confident in my capacity to cope with any problems. | − | ? | + |
| 12e. My trainers have high expectations of me. | − | ? | + |

Total

### Informal Learning

| | | | |
|---|---|---|---|
| 12a. I believed that I was capable of achieving my learning goals. | − | ? | + |
| 12b. I was sure that I could meet the challenges I set myself. | − | ? | + |
| 12c. I was confident I could complete my learning project. | − | ? | + |
| 12d. I knew I could cope with any problems that I ran into. | − | ? | + |
| 12e. I had high expectations of myself. | − | ? | + |

Total

# BELIEF

## Key Points

- We are unlikely even to attempt to learn unless we believe we can. Self-belief, self-esteem and self-confidence are all crucial to learning. And these are influenced by other people's belief or lack of belief in us.*

- Belief does not mean expecting the impossible. It has to be based on a realistic estimate of what we are capable of. And we do differ in our abilities, though the differences in the kinds or types of abilities we have are as important as the differences in level.

- In any one field of human activity, there will be people who perform better or achieve more than others. But the range of those activities and the abilities they tap is enormous. People may be good at maths, languages, computing, drawing, playing the guitar, football, chairing meetings, fixing cars, parenting, caring for old people, selling, running an office, designing houses, cooking, writing novels . . . the list is endless. Self-belief is partly a matter of identifying your own strengths, of finding the right niche or line.

- It is also based on the simple fact that most people achieve less than they could and operate somewhere below their 'ceiling'. There are many reasons for this, some of which go back to childhood and early education, which do not always provide a good start. Lack of motivation and sheer laziness may also be the cause. But given the right stimulus, help and environment, many people achieve far more than they thought they ever could. There are countless examples of this in adult education, including the Open University.

✉ **To what extent do you think you have fulfilled your potential so far in terms of learning? Ring your response.**

| | | | | |
|---|---|---|---|---|
| hardly at all | a little | partly | quite a lot | almost completely |

- Our self-belief reflects what others say about us. If a parent or a teacher consistently praises or knocks our work, that will raise or lower our expectations. The same goes for anyone else whose opinion we value, such as partners, friends or colleagues.

- Repeated failure at school is very difficult to get over, because it reinforces the message time and again, until it becomes set in concrete. One of the main tasks that teachers and trainers sometimes have therefore is to turn this self-concept round: it can be done.

- The opposite problem – over-confidence – is less common but it does occur, particularly with more experienced or senior people. Again, it needs careful analysis. Where does it come from in the first place? Does it prevent you taking on board criticism or new ideas? Is it in fact a kind of defence? Are you actually worried underneath, and trying to put on a show?

- The general climate in a group or organisation also affects our self-concept. Team managers know how it influences performance in sports: football commentators talk about 'heads dropping'. Managers talk about promoting a 'can-do' attitude in an organisation.

## ✉ Personal Notes

---

# Action

Are you generally a fairly confident type, or more hesitant and unsure of yourself? **How would your friends describe you?**

**Make a list of things in your past** which you think have affected your general image of yourself, and that may help you to understand the way you are now. Did you suffer important knocks or set-backs at some point? Can you put any lack of self-belief down to some key events? Or does it seem to be part of your personality, the way you have always been?

☺   Most people are confident in some things and not others. Divide a page into two columns and in one write down those activities which **you feel you can cope with well**

☹   and in the other column list **those which you find difficult or daunting.** Include any sort of situation or activity, large or small.

Is there a pattern? Are you happier dealing with certain kinds of work or situation than others? Certain sorts of tasks or problems?

Where does education and training fit into this list? Do you see it as one of your strengths or weaknesses? Are there particular reasons for this, for example in your **previous experience of school?**

Within education and training, are there **particular subjects or fields** which you are less confident about? Some people have mental blocks about certain subjects and panic when faced by them, e.g. maths, computing, languages. (See **Tips for the Terrified**.) But even if you don't have a complete block, is your confidence low in some fields? Again, is there a history to this? Did you have an ogre as a maths teacher? Was your French or woodwork held up to public ridicule?

The next question is: **are you doing the right subjects/topics?** (This goes back to **Course**, Section 1.) We shouldn't always stick to subjects or tasks we find easy or congenial, otherwise we would never broaden our range and might miss out on some new areas altogether. And most subjects have parts which we like and parts we don't. But if you feel you are basically in the wrong field or area, then you need to think through the reasons and get advice.

Even if you are doing the right subject or course, self-belief has to translate into action to make a difference. Do you turn your expectations into activity? It is important to develop a **regular pattern of study**, including work on your own, and to stick to it. Learning is a **habit** which you have got to develop. How much time do you put in? Do you need to increase it?

Try going over in your own mind things you have done well in any area of your life, not just education or training. For example, some people who have under-achieved at school have become very successful in their jobs. Others possess social and personal skills which go unrecognised in the education system. Others are good at music or gardening or sport. This kind of '**mental rehearsal**' will stop you running yourself down. If you can do some things well, why not others?

Finally, this is another aspect of your learning where 'it's good to talk' (OK, *it's a cliché, but true*). You may find that others actually have **the same worries or fears as you do**; strangers can look supremely confident from the outside! You may get a more realistic picture of your own strengths and weaknesses. And, as you talk about these issues, you can begin to 'excavate' your own learning history, and understand better where you are coming from.

## ✉ Belief: what should I do?

# 13 Motivation
## wanting to learn

**Sixth Form**

| | | | |
|---|---|---|---|
| 13a. I am enthusiastic about the subjects I am doing. | − | ? | + |
| 13b. I put as much effort into my work as I should. | − | ? | + |
| 13c. I have no problems focusing on my work. | − | ? | + |
| 13d. I stick at my work even when it is difficult. | − | ? | + |
| 13e. Motivation is not a problem for me. | − | ? | + |

Total

**Further Education**

| | | | |
|---|---|---|---|
| 13a. I am enthusiastic about my course. | − | ? | + |
| 13b. I put as much effort into my work as I should. | − | ? | + |
| 13c. I have no problems focusing on my work. | − | ? | + |
| 13d. I stick at my work even when it is hard. | − | ? | + |
| 13e. I have no problems with motivation. | − | ? | + |

Total

**Higher Education**

| | | | |
|---|---|---|---|
| 13a. I am enthusiastic about my degree course. | − | ? | + |
| 13b. I put as much effort into my work as I should. | − | ? | + |
| 13c. I have no problems focusing on my studies. | − | ? | + |
| 13d. I persevere with my studies even when they are difficult. | − | ? | + |
| 13e. Motivation is not a problem for me. | − | ? | + |

Total

**Training and Development**

| | | | |
|---|---|---|---|
| 13a. I am enthusiastic about the training programme. | − | ? | + |
| 13b. I put as much effort into the training as I should. | − | ? | + |
| 13c. I have no problems focusing on my training. | − | ? | + |
| 13d. I stick at my training even when it is challenging. | − | ? | + |
| 13e. My level of motivation remains high. | − | ? | + |

Total

**Informal Learning**

| | | | |
|---|---|---|---|
| 13a. I was enthusiastic about my learning project. | − | ? | + |
| 13b. I put as much effort into my project as necessary. | − | ? | + |
| 13c. I had no problems focusing on my learning project. | − | ? | + |
| 13d. I did not let any problems put me off. | − | ? | + |
| 13e. I was motivated enough to complete my project. | − | ? | + |

Total

# MOTIVATION

---

## Key Points

- Even if we can learn, we don't unless we want to. That is why this topic is so important. There are various ways of looking at motivation.*

- One is in terms of *level*. So we talk about high or low motivation, the amount of energy we put into a task. Like an engine: indeed, people talk about working at full throttle (or idling).

- Another way to think about motivation is in terms of *priorities*. We have to choose learning in preference to all the other things that we might do, e.g. socialising with friends, watching TV, earning money. Even at the basic level of concentration, learning has to compete with all the other external and internal stimuli that may be there. Our consciousness is like a marketplace with everyone trying to catch our attention.

- Other theories emphasise *internal factors* such as curiosity or sense of achievement. Others again see motivation in terms of *hierarchies of needs*, e.g. only when we have met our basic needs (thirst, hunger, security) do we want to satisfy higher level ones, such as belonging, esteem or fulfilment. Finally, some theories stress the influence of *external factors* on motivation such as reward, punishment, or simply being ignored.

In practice, motivation often seems to involve a mixture of different factors.

✉ **Pause at this point. Which of these views of motivation makes most sense to you? Can you relate any of them to your own experience?**

- Motivation is often plural rather than singular. We do things for a package of reasons rather than just one, and this applies to learning as to much else. Motivation can also change over time. You might begin a course because your friends are doing it, continue because you become interested in the subject, and complete it because you want to get a job in that field.

- Teachers and trainers vary in their attitude to motivation. Some see it as part of their job to enthuse or inspire you. Others, especially in further or higher education, argue that, since you are an adult, it is your own responsibility. No one forces you to go to college or university, so arguably it is up to you whether you work hard or not. On the other hand, learning can be difficult, and three years is a long time, with many ups and downs.

- **Informal** learners have to be self-motivated, otherwise they would not embark on their projects at all. And often success or failure in one project can mean the difference between going on to another one or stopping there. But even in this, other people can have an influence, particularly in giving a bit of encouragement if one feels low.

## ✉ Personal Notes

## Action

What you do about motivation depends on what kind of problem it is.

### Concentration

The most basic way in which a lack of motivation shows up is **concentration**. One useful tip is to make a note every time you become aware that your mind is wandering. For example, if you are reading a book or listening to the teacher, and you suddenly think about what happened at a party or realise that you need to buy some eggs, write down 'party' or 'eggs' in the margin and circle it. The next time this happens, do it again. After a week, look at all the notes you have made, and see if they fall into any one of four categories:

- **distractions** such as nearby noises or movements

- **plans** about what you are going to do

- **memories** of what has happened recently

- **anxieties** or 'unfinished business' which keeps coming back.

The mere fact of being able to label these things will make you better able to catch your mind the next time it sets off.

Lack of concentration may also be due to 'automaticity'. Our minds are constructed to switch off **anything that becomes too repetitive or routine**. This can happen in a boring lecture, but also when we read a book: because we know how to read, we go on 'automatic pilot' and read a page without taking anything in. (Probably with this book too!) The answer is to stop, take a break, and start afresh. If this keeps happening, you may simply be too tired, and it is better to change to something else or stop altogether. Some people find that **switching between different tasks** helps maintain concentration, simply because of the variety. Others prefer to focus on just one. Find out what works for you.

Wider problems of motivation need a more thoughtful analysis. You may for example feel that you are merely jumping through hoops or going through the motions: that your learning is not real. This could be because you are approaching it in terms of **memorising rather than understanding**: simply trying to reproduce the words or information without getting to grips with the meaning, what is sometimes called 'surface' rather than 'deep' learning.* (See **Understanding**, Section 17).Think about your approach; is it the right one for the course?

If you started the course with high hopes and have **gradually become disillusioned**, it may be more to do with the teaching or peer group than yourself. Try to discuss your feelings with one or two others in the group to see if they have the same reactions. You may be able to do something about it as a group, or at least support one another.

Even if the course is boring, you may get a **useful qualification** at the end of it. And even if it is useless, you may find the subject interesting or derive a **sense of achievement** from mastering it. There are usually some positive elements in the situation, and you should hang on to these.

If it all seems too daunting, try **breaking down your work into small tasks or stages**, and focus on completing the first one. When you have done that, move on to the next. Don't look too far ahead; just concentrate on making a little progress each time.

Don't be surprised if sometimes you feel you are getting nowhere (a '**learning plateau**') or even going backwards ('**unlearning**'). Learning is not always a positive or progressive experience; it can feel quite negative at times. But that is part of the overall process.

Remember: most people experience **ups and downs** of motivation, especially over the duration of a longer course. That's normal. It is only when motivation becomes a persistent problem that you need to address it.

⊠  Motivation: what should I do?

# PART C: PROCESSES

Now we get into the learning process in more depth, and look at the foundations of your learning, your sense of direction, the tasks you are given, and the
kinds of input and feedback you get. We also explore how well you understand
what you are doing and how far it opens up new ideas and approaches for you.

📖 Since you are about halfway through the book now, back off from it for a bit,
and think about what you have read and written. And about what general
changes, if any, this points towards in the way you manage your learning.

📖 When you have finished **Feedback** (Section 20), go back to some of the
sections in Part C where you scored +3 or more, making notes if you wish. Does
anything you read there make you want to alter your responses to the
questionnaire?

PART C: PROCESSES

# 14 Foundations
## prior learning and experience

**Sixth Form**

14a. My previous studies prepared me for what I am learning now.    −  ?  +
14b. I have a solid foundation for the subjects I am doing.    −  ?  +
14c. There were no major gaps in what I studied before.    −  ?  +
14d. My current course started in the right place for me.    −  ?  +
14e. What I am learning now builds on what I learned before.    −  ?  +

Total

**Further Education**

14a. My previous work equipped me for what I am learning now.    −  ?  +
14b. I have a solid foundation for the course I am doing now.    −  ?  +
14c. There were no major gaps in what I did before.    −  ?  +
14d. My current course started in the right place for me.    −  ?  +
14e. What I am learning now builds on what I learned before.    −  ?  +

Total

**Higher Education**

14a. My previous studies prepared me well for my degree course.    −  ?  +
14b. I have a solid foundation for my degree studies.    −  ?  +
14c. There were no major gaps in my previous knowledge or skills.    −  ?  +
14d. The course started in the right place for me.    −  ?  +
14e. What I am learning now builds on what I learned before.    −  ?  +

Total

**Training and Development**

14a. I was well equipped to follow this training programme.    −  ?  +
14b. My prior knowledge and skills gave me a good foundation.    −  ?  +
14c. The programme builds on my existing know-how.    −  ?  +
14d. The programme started at the right place for me.    −  ?  +
14e. What I am learning now builds on what I learned before.    −  ?  +

Total

**Informal Learning**

14a. I was well equipped to carry out my learning project.    −  ?  +
14b. I had all the necessary prior knowledge and skills.    −  ?  +
14c. I knew where to begin with my project.    −  ?  +
14d. There were no serious gaps in my existing knowledge
and skills.    −  ?  +
14e. I was able to build on what I had learned before.    −  ?  +

Total

# FOUNDATIONS

## Key Points

- New learning does not always build on old learning. Sometimes we start on a new subject or topic from scratch. But most of the learning we do builds in some way on our existing knowledge and skills, and that is why it is important to ask about foundations: the basis or baseline for our learning.

- The point becomes most obvious when the foundations are shaky. Sometimes we realise when we have begun a new course or programme that we are simply not properly equipped to follow it. There may be gaps in our prior learning, holes which should have been filled in and weren't. Perhaps we simply did not cover X or Y. And unfortunately the teacher or trainer assumes that we did, and we can feel a bit foolish admitting our ignorance.

**Does this ring a bell? If so, when did it happen?**

- Before starting, teachers and trainers should discover what their students' baseline is, and take that as their point of departure. But they often don't, either because they assume they know already, or because they feel under pressure of time and want to get on with things. And even if they do find out, it may be difficult to cater for the variety of backgrounds in a mixed group.

- Surprisingly, this problem is sometimes worse in the education system than it is in training. Trainers running one-off sessions know they can't take too much for granted and so usually make an effort to find out what people know and where they are coming from, for example by brainstorming the topic or giving a diagnostic test. But teachers and lecturers can all too easily assume that the topic was covered in the previous year, because that is what the syllabus says.

- The worst foundation problems usually occur when you move from one level of study to another, e.g. craft to technician, GCSE to A level, A level to degree. These are the fault lines in the system, and there can be major shifts or changes of gear when you cross them. The problem can also arise even at the same level if you move from one school or college to another.

- In a modular system, the problem is due to the fact that different students may have done different modules previously, and there is no real common baseline for the current module. This is the price of choice. It is difficult for staff to tailor their course to a mixed group of students, and they often have to spend the first session trying to establish common ground.

- People who teach languages, computing, maths and other subjects which involve progressive skills are often more systematic about diagnosis and pre-testing than other teachers or trainers, simply because they know the problems that can result if they don't. 'Sequencing' is an issue in all subjects: what is the best order or 'logic' for learning? But the problem is sharpest in subjects which have a strict linear sequence, where you cannot understand C until you have mastered A and B.

---

Is your subject more like

     **THIS**          **OR**          **THIS?**

    → → → → →          ↘ ↑ ↙ ↗
    → → → → →          ↙ → ← →
                       ↗ ↓ ↖ ↘

---

- A different kind of problem arises when the new learning not merely fails to build on old learning, but actually contradicts or reverses it. For example, if you have taught yourself some skill, such as playing golf or the guitar, and then decide to go and get proper lessons, you may find that you actually have to unlearn the techniques you have developed.

- The process of 'unlearning' is most common in the training field, but can happen in more academic disciplines too, where you find that what you were taught at GCSE is partly undone by A levels, which in turn is called into question in your first year at university. And the problem is perhaps most acute in mid-career education and training where people have to review and maybe abandon existing habits, approaches and attitudes. It can be quite painful and disorientating to have to retool or reinvent yourself in this way, not least because you will probably have invested quite a lot of pride and self-esteem in the way you do things. But sometimes you have to unlearn before you can relearn.

## ✉ Personal Notes

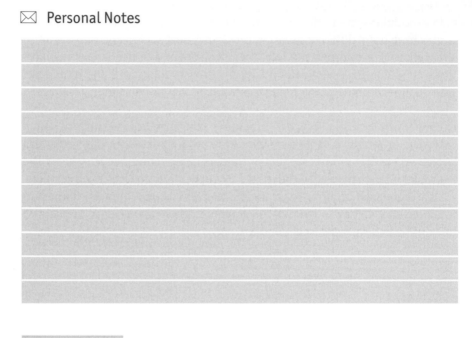

## Action

If you think your foundations are shaky for some reason, don't just leave the problem and hope it will go away. If anything, it will get worse as you get further and further into the course. You should **act now**, and try to get help. It is not your fault that you did not cover the topic.

**The first step is to ask the teacher/trainer**. Explain the problem, and see what he or she suggests. Teachers and trainers would much rather you were up-front about this than trying to hide the problem; and it is not always easy for them to diagnose individual difficulties in a large group.

You may be able to get additional or remedial teaching in certain **basic skills such as maths, computing and writing**. Many institutions now offer top-up courses in such subjects, partly because people may not have done them for some time, and need to brush up their competence.

Alternatively, there may be some '**self-help**' **books or software** that you can work on in your own time. A librarian or bookshop assistant should be able to advise you.

If you have a long summer or other break, use some of it to do basic preparation and **pre-reading** for the course to get yourself up to speed.

You may think that you lack the necessary foundations, but **don't underestimate your existing knowledge and skills**, especially if you have acquired these through experience rather than formal study. If this is the case, divide a page into three columns, as follows. In the first, list the main things you have done in the last five years (Experience). In the second, list what you think you have learned from doing those things (Learning). In the third, list what parts of the course this learning may correspond to (Topics). You may find that you have learned several things from each experience, and that some of this learning cuts across several experiences (e.g. managing time/money/people).

| EXPERIENCE | LEARNING | TOPICS |
|---|---|---|
| Xxxxxxx | Xxxxxxx | |
| | Xxxxxxx | Xxxxxx |
| Xxxxxxx | Xxxxxxx | |
| | Xxxxxxx | Xxxxxxx |
| | Xxxxxxx | |
| | Xxxxxxx | Xxxxxxx |
| Xxxxxxx | Xxxxxxx | |
| | Xxxxxxx | Xxxxxxx |

If you think that you already know some of what the course covers, and don't need to go over the ground again, ask if you can get some exemptions or 'advanced standing' on the basis of AP(E)L: **Accreditation of Prior (Experiential) Learning**. You will need to make a claim and provide evidence along the lines of the three columns above.

Trainers should identify the '**training gap**' between what you can already do and what you need to be able to do, but you should also try to analyse this yourself, since they may not have enough information about your prior expertise.

✉ Foundations: what should I do?

# 15 Orientation

## knowing where you are going

**Sixth Form**

15a. I know what to aim for in each subject.  — ? +
15b. I know where I am going in each subject.  — ? +
15c. I know where I am with my studies.  — ? +
15d. The structure of the course is clear.  — ? +
15e. I am clear about what I need to learn.  — ? +

Total

**Further Education**

15a. I know what to aim for in my course.  — ? +
15b. I know where I am going in my course.  — ? +
15c. I know where I am with my studies.  — ? +
15d. The structure of the course is clear.  — ? +
15e. I am clear about what I need to learn.  — ? +

Total

**Higher Education**

15a. I know what to aim for in my degree course.  — ? +
15b. I know where I am going on my degree course.  — ? +
15c. I know where I am with my studies.  — ? +
15d. The structure of the course is clear.  — ? +
15e. I am clear about what I need to learn.  — ? +

Total

**Training and Development**

15a. I am clear about the objectives of the programme.  — ? +
15b. I know where I am going on the programme.  — ? +
15c. I can see how the different parts of the programme
        fit together.  — ? +
15d. I know where I am on the programme.  — ? +
15e. I am clear about what I need to learn.  — ? +

Total

**Informal Learning**

15a. I knew what to aim for in my learning project.  — ? +
15b. I had enough sense of direction in my learning project.  — ? +
15c. I knew generally where I was going with my learning project.  — ? +
15d. I structured my learning project well.  — ? +
15e. I was clear enough about what I needed to learn.  — ? +

Total

# ORIENTATION

---

## Key Points

- We often learn better if we have some sense of direction, some feel for what we are aiming at. This allows us to be selective in what we pay attention to, and to focus our energies and activities. This is what we mean by orientation here: knowing where you are and where you are trying to get to. The opposite is the feeling that you have lost the plot.

✉ **Pause at this point. What do YOU feel?**

- Not all learning has clear aims. For example, when we learn **informally**, we often work stage by stage, and one thing leads to another. The answer to one problem becomes the question for the next. This kind of 'incremental' learning is perfectly OK; we do not always need some overall goal or plan. Like a lot of the rest of our lives, learning can be evolutionary or opportunistic, and we develop our goals and plans as we go along. Improvisation can be a positive thing, and may be as important as planning.

- Even in formal courses, learning may develop in this kind of way. This is because learning itself changes our perception of aims. At the start of a course, we may think that certain topics are priorities, but when we get further into it we may realise that they are not actually very important, and that the course is really about something else. In education and training, the goal-posts tend to move depending on where you look at them from.

- The main way in which teachers and trainers provide orientation is through lists of aims and objectives. Aims may be quite general and provide a 'broad steer'. They signal the general expectations of the course. Objectives are more specific and precise and spell out what you should be able to do, under what conditions, and to what level. You may also come across the words 'competences' or 'outcomes' which mean roughly the same, though the first is usually related to work/employment.

- A lot depends on the subject and level of study. It is much easier to spell out objectives in technical and vocational subjects than in more academic ones. The further you go up the educational or training ladder, the more open-ended things tend to become (something which can give you a sense of vertigo!). By contrast, training and development programmes usually have quite specific objectives which are related to staff and organisational needs.

- Most formal courses these days have lists of aims and objectives or outcomes. This emphasis often stems from the need to assess people, as distinct from teach them. How can you judge someone's performance if you don't know what he or she was aiming at in the first place? However, a course may also have important 'unintended outcomes' or side-effects/spin-offs, and these can be positive or negative. One negative outcome might be that you never want to go near the subject again.

- And people vary in the amount of structure and direction they want. What to one individual will be reassuring signposts will feel like travel restrictions to another. Is there too much or too little orientation for your taste?

- Do you have clear personal goals, or are you hoping that the course will help you sort them out? Are you doing it because you are not quite sure what else to do? That is quite a common situation, and you shouldn't blame yourself for not having everything worked out in advance. Some people have a definite educational and career pathway mapped out, but the relationship between education and employment is quite flexible in other cases, and doing a broad or non-vocational course can equip you with some of the generic knowledge and skills – the capacity to analyse problems, evaluate evidence, make judgements, think for yourself – that many employers say they want.

Make some notes below on your own situation.

✉ Personal Notes

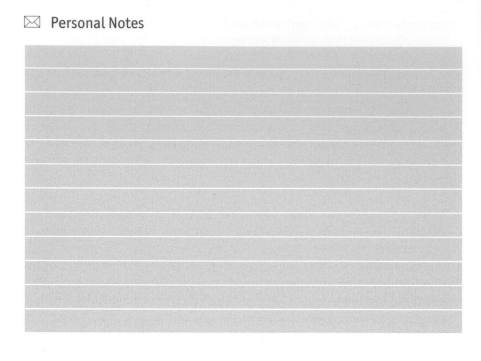

---

# Action

**It is normal to feel a bit disorientated at the beginning** of a course, so give it and yourself some time. But if the feeling persists, check with your friends whether they are feeling the same way. You can pick up some prior orientation from **people who have done the course before**, subject to the 'health warnings' mentioned earlier: they may have had a different experience.

If you do feel a bit lost or at sea, **read the course documentation** (prospectus, syllabus, handbooks, outlines, etc.) again. You may have missed things, or not read it properly the first time. Think about what it actually means, and try to decode any bits that are not clear. If necessary, ask staff for clarification.

You can also try to get hold of **past assessment tests or questions** (though access to these will be restricted on some courses). They will give you a concrete idea of expected outcomes, but check that the pattern has not changed in the mean time. Few courses remain exactly the same from one round to the next.

Orientation is not a one-off thing that happens only at the beginning of a course or programme. You may need to 'check your position' several times, to make sure you are still heading in the right direction, especially on a longer course with modular options. That may involve talking to your **tutor or supervisor**.

If you feel confused in the middle of the course, you can try **drawing a map** of how the various parts of it relate to one another in your mind. And perhaps compare that with someone else's.

One problem with lists of objectives and outcomes is to find out if they are all equally important. Probably they aren't, but staff will usually say they that they are, since they don't want you to focus on only some parts of the topic. **Listen out for hints, clues, cues as to what is most important**. If you feel you are not picking up enough about what is going on, perhaps you need to spend more time socialising with other people on the course.

Orientation can be a problem **not just at the beginning of a course but at the end**, when you suddenly feel lost without the routine of study and company of friends. So it is important to begin thinking about what to do after the course while you are still on it. And that may involve working out where you are going in the longer term, perhaps with the help of a **careers service or office**. While these tended to deal only with young people in the past, they are geared to adults now as well. Career development for those already in work is usually handled within the organisation, although you can get external advice as well, at a price.

## ✉ Orientation: what should I do?

# 16  Input

## content and coverage

**Sixth Form**

16a.  I like the content of each subject.                                 − ? +
16b.  Each subject covers the right ground.                               − ? +
16c.  I get all the input I need in each subject.                         − ? +
16d.  I find each subject stimulating.                                    − ? +
16e.  I am getting a lot out of each subject.                             − ? +

        Total


**Further Education**

16a.  I like the content of the course.                                   − ? +
16b.  The course covers the right ground.                                 − ? +
16c.  I get all the input I need from the course.                         − ? +
16d.  I find the course stimulating.                                      − ? +
16e.  I am getting a lot out of the course.                               − ? +

        Total


**Higher Education**

16a.  I like the content of the course.                                   − ? +
16b.  The course covers the right ground.                                 − ? +
16c.  I get all the input I need from the course.                         − ? +
16d.  I find the course stimulating.                                      − ? +
16e.  I am getting a lot out of the course.                               − ? +

        Total


**Training and Development**

16a.  I like the content of the programme.                                − ? +
16b.  The programme covers the right ground.                              − ? +
16c.  I get all the input I need from the programme.                      − ? +
16d.  I find the programme stimulating.                                   − ? +
16e.  I am getting a lot out of the programme.                            − ? +

        Total


**Informal Learning**

16a.  I knew what information I needed to get.                             − ? +
16b.  I got all the information I needed.                                  − ? +
16c.  I got all the inputs necessary for my project.                      − ? +
16d.  I found my project stimulating.                                     − ? +
16e.  I got a lot out of doing my project.                                − ? +

        Total

# INPUT

---

## Key Points

- One way of thinking about learning is in terms of inputs, processing and outputs. You receive inputs from various sources (teachers, materials, peers), process the information these contain, and then output the results in what you say and write, in the form of answers to questions, classroom tasks, assignments, exams and performance. This is a rather crude model, but it does highlight the fact that without some initial input, you would have nothing to learn.

- This section focuses on the inputs from teachers/trainers and materials; the inputs from your peers in the group have been covered already under **Interaction** (Section 9). Inputs can come in various forms: not only the obvious ones of talk (presentations, lectures, briefings) and reading (handouts, books, articles, software) but also through demonstration (in practical or laboratory classes) or organised workshops, which may involve simulations, case studies and role plays. All these give you information (in the broadest sense) to work on.

- There are three basic questions.

  ⇨ First, is the *content* OK? Is it substantial enough, or is the course a bit thin? Does it cover what it should, or are there gaps? Is it accurate and up-to-date? Do the teachers/trainers know their stuff?

  ⇨ Second, is it *put across well*? Are the presentations clear and well organised? Can you follow what staff say? Are the course materials well designed and user-friendly?

  ⇨ Third, *do you make good use* of all these inputs? Do you do the reading before or afterwards? Do you draw on the available materials? Do you take adequate notes?

- Sometimes the problem is that there is simply too much input, too much to cover in the time. A lot of courses are very full, simply because people keep adding new topics without getting rid of older ones. This can lead to information overload, leaving you too little time to absorb what is being given to you, and reducing you to memorising rather than understanding.

- Don't assume that all the inputs have to come from the teacher or trainer. Participants – and you yourself – can bring a lot to courses and programmes, particularly in continuing education and training, where there may be a great deal of knowledge and expertise already in the group. The job of the teacher is to incorporate this. Does this happen, or is this kind of contribution disregarded or downgraded in favour of the formal, official input?

- The input–process–output model is seen most clearly in skill learning, which is most common in vocational and technical courses, but also occurs in other professional fields such as medicine, nursing and law. (The most common examples are driving and computing.) If you are involved in skill learning you will probably recognise the following stages:*

  ⇨ *Demonstration*: someone shows you how to do it, usually with some background explanation and verbal cues (*watch how I . . . this is the tricky bit . . .* )

  ⇨ *Practice*: you start to practise the skill yourself, sometimes in parts, with guidance and feedback from the teacher/instructor, gradually eliminating errors and putting it all together

  ⇨ *Automation*: you continue to practise mainly under your own steam, increasing your speed and precision and decreasing your conscious effort to the point where you can begin to do it 'without thinking'

  ⇨ *Variation*: once you are reasonably secure, you learn to build in changes to the pattern and to cope with the unexpected, including things going wrong

  ⇨ *Transfer*: you learn how to apply the essential elements of the skill to different tasks, equipment or situations.

If you experience any problems with skill learning, try to work out which of the above stages they relate to, remembering that there may be some overlap between them. A lot will depend on the nature of the skill, and the context you have to perform it in, with time pressure often a key factor.

⊠    **Any problems at any stage?**

Now make notes on any other aspects of **input** in your learning. Refer back to the three basic questions above.

⊠    Personal Notes

## Action

Some input problems go beyond the immediate course, and there may not be much you can do about them. If there is a basic lack of materials or equipment, the problem may stem from lack of funding. However, institutions usually have **small pots of money** here and there, and if you (and others) can make a good case for some extra books or computers or other materials, they may be able to find some.

Equally, if there is a **set syllabus or programme** which has been laid down by some official body, there is little you can do. National curricula, programme specifications or professional regulations may dictate the pattern. However, even within this, individual teachers/trainers may have some discretion about the order they do things in or how much emphasis they place on each topic.

If you find the materials too difficult, ask if there are some **basic texts** which you can use on your own. In the schools sector, **revision guides** are available, and there is a lot of material on the **World Wide Web**, though be careful: it varies in quality. If you find the course too easy or undemanding, ask for some more advanced or additional material. Staff will usually be pleased at this, since it shows you are keen.

**If the problems lie with the individual teacher/trainer** (poor preparation/ delivery/handouts, etc.) it is best to discuss these with your peers before you approach the person. Staff can be touchy about criticism, and it is better coming from a number of people rather than just you. On many courses and programmes, there will be feedback forms, but the trouble is that these are only likely to benefit the next group. But the same rules apply as when staff give learners feedback: find some positive things to say as well, and suggest constructive changes or ways forward.

If you cannot get much change out of staff, your only option is to **work together with your friends** to try to compensate for any staff weaknesses. Go through the materials together, and try to make sense of them yourselves.

## Reading and Note-Taking

Input involves two important skills on your side. First, think about how you **read**. Don't just start automatically at page 1 and plough through the whole text. First, skim through the book and get an overview of it: look at the table of contents, section headings, summaries, the beginnings and ends of chapters. Apart from anything else, this will give you a mental framework within which you can house the detailed information. Then decide whether you need to (a) discard the book, (b) read some parts properly, or (c) read the entire text in depth. There is more than one way of reading a book or text, so it is important to think about your **reading strategies**. A book is a store of information, and you can extract information from it in various ways.

Second, **look at the way you take notes** and bear in mind four points:

- There is no need to write full sentences, or redo a fair copy afterwards: think of notes as text messages which you are sending to yourself and will receive in several weeks'/months' time. They must make sense, but don't worry about writing proper English.

- Use abbreviations wherever possible, and develop your own 'code' for common words (such as because/different from/leading to). This will save you time.

- Don't cram every page full: space helps to give a sense of structure and emphasis (think of advertisements). Use numbering, headings, arrows, etc. to shape the meaning.

- Spend a little time (a 'chink', see p. 25) going through your notes not too long afterwards. This will help to fix them in your mind, and ensure that you actually understand what you have written ('*it made sense at the time . . .*')

As usual, the **informal** learner has to find his or her own inputs. But **other people** can be a great help in pointing you in the right direction, though the **Web** is increasingly useful also in locating materials (but you may have to wade through a good deal to find what you really want). If you don't know how to use it, ask someone to show you. It's not difficult once you get the hang of it.

## ✉ Input: what should I do?

# 17 Understanding
## following what you are learning

**Sixth Form**

17a. Each of my subjects makes sense to me.    − ? +
17b. I can follow what we are doing in each subject.    − ? +
17c. The teachers are good at explaining things.    − ? +
17d. I understand what I am learning.    − ? +
17e. I could explain the subject-matter to another student.    − ? +

     Total

**Further Education**

17a. The course makes sense to me.    − ? +
17b. I can follow what we are doing in each part of the course.    − ? +
17c. The lecturers are good at explaining things.    − ? +
17d. I understand what I am learning.    − ? +
17e. I could explain the course content to another student.    − ? +

     Total

**Higher Education**

17a. The course makes sense to me.    − ? +
17b. I can follow what we are doing in each part of the course.    − ? +
17c. The lecturers are good at explaining things.    − ? +
17d. I have a good understanding of what I am learning.    − ? +
17e. I could explain the subject-matter to another student.    − ? +

     Total

**Training and Development**

17a. The programme makes sense to me.    − ? +
17b. I can follow what we are doing on the programme.    − ? +
17c. The trainers are good at explaining things.    − ? +
17d. I believe I am mastering what I am learning.    − ? +
17e. I could explain the topics to another participant.    − ? +

     Total

**Informal Learning**

17a. My learning project made sense to me.    − ? +
17b. I was able to figure things out for myself.    − ? +
17c. I was able to master each stage of my project.    − ? +
17d. There were people who could explain things to me
     if necessary.    − ? +
17e. I could explain what I learned to someone else now.    − ? +

     Total

# UNDERSTANDING

## Key Points

- To some extent, learning is a matter of memorising and reproducing what you have learned. There is a factual element in all subjects, and it is larger and more important in some than others. So, depending on what course you are doing, you may have to spend some time absorbing information, vocabulary, definitions, formulae, equations, regulations, procedures and so on.

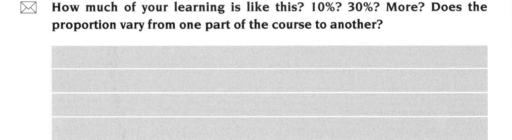 **How much of your learning is like this? 10%? 30%? More? Does the proportion vary from one part of the course to another?**

- Sheer repetition or practice is the main way to learn such information; going over it again and again until it has gone in. But you will find that if you can attach meanings to some of it, you will remember it more easily. So you might associate a word with a picture, sound or situation, or make certain headings into an acronym which spells something (e.g. **SWOT** in **Course**, Section 1).

- These little tricks contain an important truth, which is that most learning has to be meaningful. It has to make sense to you; you need to understand it. Our minds seem to discard information which is purely random or meaningless, and continually search for pattern and coherence.

- Do you feel that you really understand what you are learning? Have you mastered it properly? The key test is: *could you teach it to someone else? Could you pass it on?*

- There are various reasons why people sometimes learn without under- standing. To begin with, the course may be so full that you don't really have time to digest it properly. The moment you finish one topic, you are on to the next, without any opportunity for reflection and assimilation.

• Or the teacher/trainer may not be good at explaining things, or have forgotten what it is like not to understand, or be in too much of a hurry, or have too large a group, or simply lack the patience.

• You might also lack the confidence to ask questions, or feel foolish in front of the group. However, the chances are that if you don't understand, other people won't either.

• Your previous schooling or experience may have involved a lot of memorising, especially if there was a more traditional approach. Nowadays there is rather more emphasis on understanding and application in both courses and assessment. But check with your teacher/trainer what the assessment criteria are, and be guided by him or her.

## ✉ Personal Notes

# Action

*Learning is demanding.* Ideas are slippery, arguments complex, skills difficult to master, problems hard to solve and even harder to identify. So it is normal to have to struggle to figure out what something means, to work out new ways of doing things, or to develop effective skills. Having said that, you should be concerned if you really don't understand what is going on, and there are various ways you can try to tackle this. Note in the margin which ones you might use.

- **Break your work down into smaller pieces or stages**, making sure you have grasped each one properly before moving on to the next.     YES/NO

- **Try working backwards from the solution** (if you know it) as well as forwards from the problem. This may be useful with quantitative problems.     YES/NO

- **Check the accuracy and rigour of each stage** in your calculations or thinking where there is a strict linear process.     YES/NO

- **Try translating difficult concepts or terms into words which make sense to you**, but be careful not to employ these where there is a precise official or technical meaning.     YES/NO

- **Relate the concepts and arguments** to examples, situations or applications which you are familiar with.     YES/NO

- **Interpret the ideas** in the light of your own thinking or experience.     YES/NO

- **Create a map or diagram** of how all the different aspects of the topic fit together.     YES/NO

- **Brainstorm the problem**, letting it all just come out and then seeing what you have.     YES/NO

- **Try explaining/teaching it** to someone else.     YES/NO

If the teacher/trainer invites questions during the session, *ask*. If something is really unclear, you may be able to interrupt, depending on the nature of the session. Alternatively, ask him or her during the break or after the class. For a major problem, request a special appointment and say what it is about in advance in order to give the teacher time to think about it.

Have a look at the special box on **Question and Answer** overleaf.

Finally, there are reference books and revision guides in many subjects, particularly at school level, which actually **explain things in the way that teachers or trainers should but sometimes don't**. And there is lots of stuff now on the Web. But again, don't just parrot the answers, and certainly don't just download them: that is plagiarism (cheating). There are now programs designed to spot such material in essays and projects.

You can get through quite a lot of courses just by remembering and repro-ducing what you have been taught, but in the end that probably will not be enough. Not only will you forget most of the material, but you will not have internalised it in a way which allows you to build on it yourself. **That is why understanding is so important: it makes your learning your own**.

## ✉ Understanding: what should I do?

# Question and Answer

The process of question and answer (Q&A) lies at the heart of explaining and understanding, so it is important to analyse it. There are two main kinds of questions:

1  closed questions, which look for a single, right answer (When was the General Strike? What is the formula for X?)

2  open questions, which invite a range of responses (Is *Hamlet* a revenge tragedy? What are the causes of inflation?)

The process of question and answer depends both on the topic and the style of teaching, but there are certain common patterns. When you ask a teacher/trainer a question he or she may

- give you a straight answer
- answer with an example, parallel or analogy
- break the question down into parts before answering it
- reformulate or rephrase the question
- summarise it for the group
- ask you what you think
- ask other people what they think
- ask you what you mean
- ask you why you asked it
- link it to another question
- tell you they are coming to it later
- tell you they don't know (quite rare this)
- tell you that they have covered it already
- or other less helpful replies . . .

Listen to the process of Q&A and you will hear these different kinds of responses. The point is that simply giving a direct answer is not always the best way to promote learning; some of the other responses will make you think harder, and perhaps lead to a wider discussion in the group.

Turning the process round, what do YOU do when the teacher asks YOU a question?

# 18  Enquiry
## exploring and questioning

**Sixth Form**

18a. My subjects stimulate me to explore ideas.                               −  ?  +
18b. My subjects encourage me to question things.                         .     −  ?  +
18c. The subjects I am doing make me think.                                    −  ?  +
18d. My subjects are widening my horizons.                                     −  ?  +
18e. I am encouraged by the experience to go on learning.                      −  ?  +

Total

**Further Education**

18a. My course stimulates me to explore ideas.                                 −  ?  +
18b. The course encourages me to question existing practices.                  −  ?  +
18c. The course I am doing makes me think.                                      −  ?  +
18d. The course develops my capacity to solve problems.                        −  ?  +
18e. I am encouraged by the experience to go on learning.                      −  ?  +

Total

**Higher Education**

18a. My degree course stimulates me to explore ideas.                          −  ?  +
18b. The course encourages me to question assumptions.                         −  ?  +
18c. The course makes me think.                                                −  ?  +
18d. The course develops my critical capacities.                               −  ?  +
18e. I am encouraged by the experience to continue learning.                   −  ?  +

Total

**Training and Development**

18a. My programme stimulates me to explore new approaches.                     −  ?  +
18b. The programme encourages me to question existing
     practices.                                                                −  ?  +
18c. The programme I am following makes me think.                              −  ?  +
18d. The programme develops my capacity to solve problems.                     −  ?  +
18e. I am encouraged by the experience to go on learning.                      −  ?  +

Total

**Informal Learning**

18a. My learning project opened up new ideas for me.                           −  ?  +
18b. It led me to explore new approaches.                                      −  ?  +
18c. It caused me to question existing practices.                              −  ?  +
18d. My learning project made me think.                                        −  ?  +
18e. I was encouraged by my project to go on learning.                         −  ?  +

Total

# ENQUIRY

## Key Points

- A good deal of learning is a matter not simply of absorbing the information you get (see **Input**, Section 16) or even understanding it (see **Understanding**, Section 17) but of enquiry: the open-ended exploration of some topic or field. The purest form of enquiry is research, which attempts to push back the boundaries of our knowledge, and this underpins courses in higher education.

- However, even at other levels in the system, enquiry may be an important aspect of learning, not so much for its content, as for the process of thinking it involves. It is important to develop a questioning approach, not only because this stimulates us to progress to higher levels, but because many of the problems we face in work or life are new or open-ended and have no ready-made solutions.

- This is increasingly true in training and development also. In the past, training was often seen as limited and narrow compared to education, and concerned only with routine skills. Nothing could now be further from the truth. In a modern economy, work is itself more open-ended, and requires a capacity to address problems in a flexible and innovative way.

✉ **How important is enquiry in your course or project?**

| not important | quite important | important | very important |
|---|---|---|---|

- Despite what has just been said, you may find that your course is limited in terms of enquiry, and there may be good reasons for this.

  ⇨ It may have very specific objectives which it needs to focus on and achieve in a limited time. This is the case with many short training courses.

  ⇨ It may form an early stage in a longer-term process, aiming merely to lay the foundations. This may be true of subjects which require a sound knowledge base.

⇨ With arts and crafts you may have to master the techniques before you can begin thinking much about interpretation.

⇨ It may be concerned with teaching routine technical or other skills.

⇨ It may aim to develop certain disciplined attitudes and forms of behaviour.

• Enquiry may also be limited for other reasons. The course may be over-loaded leaving no time to go down interesting avenues or off on productive tangents. Teachers and trainers might like to explore different ideas and approaches but live under continual syllabus pressure to cover the ground, and so 'stick to the script'.

• Both staff and learners may be focused on assessment, which itself might not encourage an open-ended or creative approach.

• The staff themselves may be set in their ways and simply unwilling to consider unorthodox questions or approaches. They may snuff out any discussion or dissent.

• Learners may not want the uncertainty of alternative or conflicting ideas and approaches. Enquiry is high risk, by definition. We do not know what will come out of the process, and some of it will turn out to have been a waste of time.

• People may think that they know the answers already, and see no point in 'pulling things up by the roots' or 'going back to square one'. This can be particularly true with mid-career education and training. Experience is double-edged: it gives us security, but that security can turn into a prison.

• Open-ended enquiry may be limited by the professional or wider culture. Questioning may only be allowed within certain limits defined by authority or convention. Certain assumptions and values may be taken for granted and therefore 'off-limits'.

Does any of this affect you?

✉ Personal Notes

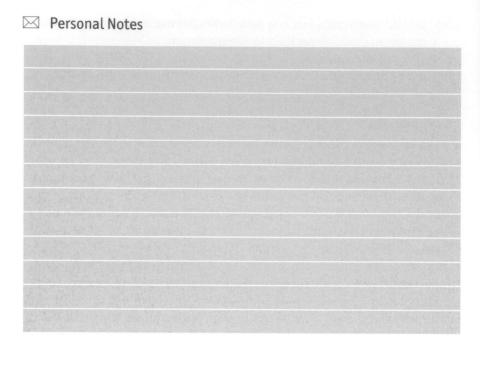

---

## Action

**The first thing is to decide what kind of course you are on**. If it emphasises enquiry, then you can do some of the things below. If it does not (and there may be good reasons for that) you may have to find other outlets for your curiosity. If you want to pursue a more enquiring approach to what you are learning, there are several things you can do.

If there is a choice, opt for **assignments** that allow you to explore alternative ideas or approaches. There may also be a project or longer piece of work at some stage which you can use in this way.

**Keep a private diary or logbook** to record your own thoughts and ideas. Don't make this too heavy-going, or you will soon give it up. An entry once or twice a week should be plenty. Note down not just what has happened but what you think and feel. Every so often, look back on what you have written and see how your own thinking has developed. Such a diary is a built-in part of some professional training courses.

**Find a few like minds** among your peers and spend time with them outside the formal sessions discussing things over coffee, etc.

Don't just stick to the syllabus or the set books. **Browse or skim** more widely: you don't have to read everything in depth. You may be surprised at what you find, and will usually earn some Brownie points as well. Try to make **cross-links** between ideas and topics which come in different 'boxes' or compartments of the course.

'Getting teacher off the subject' has always been a favourite pastime of school pupils, but don't worry if the teacher or group sometimes **go off on a tangent**. This can lead to angles and connections that would not otherwise be explored. Teaching and learning involve improvisation as well as planning, and skilled staff know how to exploit the 'teachable moment'. Think what you can do to open up such avenues (*Does this have anything to do with/I once came across an example of . . . ?*) but also to get back on track when you need to (*Can I use this in my assignment/Is this likely to come up in the exam/How does this relate back to . . . ?*)

Try **brainstorming** a topic or problem. Take a blank sheet of paper, start in the middle and simply write down anything that comes into your head about it. Don't try to be selective at this stage; take risks, go with the flow. Then have a look at what you have got, and see what you make of it. You can do this individually or as a group.

In general, be ready to ask yourself: **what is the question behind this question?** What is the assumption behind this assumption? Remember that being critical is not the same as being negative. Often things have progressed in the past only because someone has approached them critically or creatively, in a way that was rejected at first by others.

Now make notes on what you could do to change this aspect of your learning.

✉ Enquiry: what should I do?

# 19  Tasks

the work you do

**Sixth Form**

19a.  The teachers give us the right kinds of things to do.      − ? +
19b.  The classroom activities are useful.      − ? +
19c.  The homework I am set is relevant.      − ? +
19d.  I can see the point of each learning task.      − ? +
19e.  The tasks help me to get to grips with my subjects.      − ? +

Total

**Further Education**

19a.  The lecturers give us the right kinds of things to do.      − ? +
19b.  The activities in class are useful.      − ? +
19c.  The work I do outside class is useful.      − ? +
19d.  I can see the point of each learning task.      − ? +
19e.  The tasks help me to get to grips with what I am learning.      − ? +

Total

**Higher Education**

19a.  The lecturers give us the right kinds of things to do.      − ? +
19b.  The work we do in the taught sessions is useful.      − ? +
19c.  The work I do on my own is useful.      − ? +
19d.  I can see the point of the various learning tasks.      − ? +
19e.  The tasks help me get to grips with my subject.      − ? +

Total

**Training and Development**

19a.  The trainers give us the right kinds of things to do.      − ? +
19b.  The face-to-face sessions are useful.      − ? +
19c.  The tasks we are given are relevant.      − ? +
19d.  I can see the point of the various learning tasks.      − ? +
19e.  The tasks help me get to grips with what I am learning.      − ? +

Total

**Informal Learning**

19a.  I gave myself things to do in my learning project.      − ? +
19b.  I set myself tasks during my learning project.      − ? +
19c.  I chose the right kinds of learning tasks.      − ? +
19d.  Each task contributed to my learning.      − ? +
19e.  The tasks helped me get to grips with what I was learning.      − ? +

Total

# TASKS

## Key Points

- If you listen to students or trainees chatting, you will often overhear them say things like 'She sprang a vocab test on us today', 'I have to give a presentation on it tomorrow', 'Everyone's worried about the assignment' or ' I've still not written up that experiment'. All of these refer to learning tasks.

- One of the most important things that teachers and trainers do for learners is to set them tasks. Tasks are central to learning. They require us to take the inputs we get, process them and turn them into an 'output' of some kind, whether spoken, written or in some other kind of performance.

- Tasks are a key aspect of learning because they engage us actively in what we are doing. We can't just sit back passively and let it all drift over us: we have to take the information and do something with it. Different subjects require different kinds of tasks, but the key thing is our engagement in the process. Learning is a form of *doing*. It is like getting into gear in driving.

- Some tasks take place during a class or session. We have to speak or make a presentation or report on something. We are given an exercise to work on either individually or as a group. As well as the more familiar activities, classroom tasks may include case studies, role plays, simulations, experiments and mini-projects.

- Other tasks are set for homework or outside the session: reading, writing short pieces, doing exercises, practising some skill, or completing a full-scale assignment such as an essay or report. But always the purpose is the same: to get us to engage with and apply what we are learning.

- If tasks are so important, why do they sometimes not work? Why do they not fulfil their purpose?

  ⇨ One problem is that the specification of the task is vague or incomplete. People aren't clear about what they are meant to do. If so, you will probably hear them asking one another.

⇨ There may not be enough time to do it properly. Teachers and trainers sometimes underestimate how long it takes to complete the task, because they can do it already. This can be frustrating. A good teacher/trainer will check whether most people have finished or not.

⇨ There may not be the resources necessary to carry out the task. The books are all out of the library, the computer terminals are all occupied, the workshops or labs are not free, the data or materials are not available.

⇨ A more serious problem is that the task itself does not actually contribute to learning. It might be set simply to keep the class quiet, or to give people something to do. It may go over ground that has been covered before, and bore us. It may be too advanced, and lie beyond us.

✉ **Have you run into any of these problems?**

• People who are learning **informally** have to set themselves the appropriate task, not so difficult that it is beyond their reach, not so easy or familiar that it does not teach them anything new. This is quite an art, and it is the same art that the good teacher or trainer has of moving learners on to the next stage. But tasks cannot simply be dumped on people, they need some guidance about how to set about them.

• In training and development especially, tasks form a bridge between theory and practice. The right tasks teach us how to translate general ideas into concrete applications. Is that your experience, or is there still a gap between the two?

• Interpreting the task may itself be part of the task in higher levels of education and training. Questions and assignments may be deliberately broad, ambiguous or open-ended, and part of our job is to select one possible approach or angle from several. This is still good teaching/training: the task is appropriate because the world does not give us everything on a plate.

✉ Personal Notes

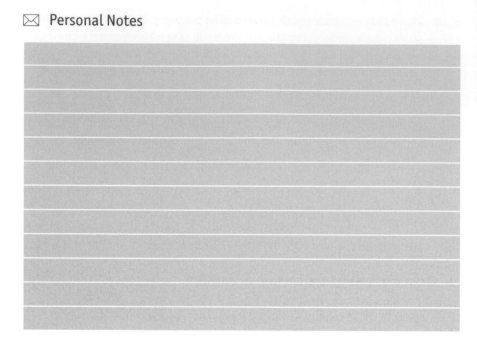

## Action

Ring your response to each of the following questions.

- **Are you clear what the task is?** YES/NO

  If not, you should ask. Better that than barking up the wrong tree. Other people may well be a bit uncertain also, even if they have not said so. If the teacher/trainer seems unapproachable or gives you the brush-off, try your friends. Or possibly someone who did the course or programme previously, though be careful: the task may have changed.

- **Are you clear about the rules?** YES/NO

  Make sure you are clear not only about the content of the task but also about the form: word limit, numbers of copies, word-processing, deadlines, etc. These practicalities are important, and you need to get them right or you may lose marks.

- **Do you need to gather materials for the task?**                    **YES/NO**

Do this beforehand so that you are not chasing around at the last minute. Get hold of what you will need. There is nothing worse than going to the library three days before and finding the book is out.

- **Is your task unfamiliar or new?**                    **YES/NO**

If so, work out how you are going to tackle it before you start. Pre-planning is important. Even though you may want to get going right away, you should spend a bit of time thinking through your strategy rather than diving straight in. This won't take long, and will pay off.

- **Does your task involve practical work or field work?**                    **YES/NO**

You need to think through the practicalities of time, cost, venues, travel, communication and so on. Build in some margin of error. Allow for slippage, particularly if it depends on other people or organisations. And have a fall-back strategy if things start to go badly wrong.

- **Does your task involve a longer piece of writing?**                    **YES/NO**

It is impossible to give general advice about how to structure essays or longer pieces of writing, since this varies from one subject and level to another, and depends very much on the title or question. **Ask your teacher/trainer**. However, some people find it useful to approach the work in two stages: first, initial brainstorming of the topic, where you put down anything that comes into your head on a sheet of paper, in the form of a map or network of ideas, and second, organising this into a consecutive plan which will form the main stages or sections of the essay. You will probably find that there are several possible structures, and that you can't cover everything. Use your introduction to explain what you are going to do and not do.

- **Are there subject conventions for presenting and writing the assignment?**                    **YES/NO**

You may have to present your task in a particular way, in terms of layout, headings, language and style. This is the case with scientific, medical and technical reports for example, and you need to know and follow these conventions. For example, you may or may not be able to use the word 'I' and there may be certain phrases which you should use or avoid.

- **Does your task involve repeated practice?**                    YES/NO

Take breaks every so often, depending on your stamina and concentration. Some skills may need to be broken down and practised in parts before being performed as a whole; others require a whole–part–whole approach. A lot depends on the nature of the skill.

- **Can you get feedback during the task?**                    YES/NO

If so, make use of it. If you are learning a skill it is especially important to get feedback regularly otherwise you may acquire bad habits or techniques which may be difficult to unlearn again. With a longer or larger piece of work such as a project, get some feedback at an early stage to make sure you are on the right track, rather than waiting until you have finished the whole thing.

- **Have you got several tasks to do at the same time?**                    YES/NO

If your course has several modules or parts, you will probably have to juggle your tasks. Try to manage your assignments so that they don't all bunch together. If you have simultaneous deadlines, stagger your work so that you get some out of the way earlier. Some people seem to prefer working on several tasks at the same time, others like to focus on one and complete it before tackling the next. Are you **multi-minded or single-minded?** Find out what is best for you.

## ✉ Tasks: what should I do?

# 20 Feedback
## knowing how you are doing

**Sixth Form**

20a. The teachers give me enough feedback on my work.     − ? +
20b. The teachers' comments are helpful.     − ? +
20c. I know how well I am doing in each subject.     − ? +
20d. I know which parts of my work I need to improve.     − ? +
20e. I am a good judge of my own progress.     − ? +

     Total

**Further Education**

20a. The lecturers give me enough feedback on my work.     − ? +
20b. The lecturers' comments are helpful.     − ? +
20c. I know how well I am doing on the course.     − ? +
20d. I know which parts of my work I need to improve.     − ? +
20e. I am a good judge of my own progress.     − ? +

     Total

**Higher Education**

20a. The lecturers give me enough feedback on my work.     − ? +
20b. The lecturers' comments are informative and constructive.     − ? +
20c. I know how well I am doing on the course.     − ? +
20d. I know which parts of my work I need to improve.     − ? +
20e. I am a good judge of my own progress.     − ? +

     Total

**Training and Development**

20a. The trainers give me enough feedback on my performance.     − ? +
20b. The trainers' comments are useful and constructive.     − ? +
20c. I get feedback from other participants on my performance.     − ? +
20d. I know the strengths and weaknesses in my work.     − ? +
20e. I can evaluate my own progress.     − ? +

     Total

**Informal Learning**

20a. I knew how to monitor my own progress.     − ? +
20b. I knew which parts of my project I needed to work on.     − ? +
20c. I was able to judge the quality of my work.     − ? +
20d. I was able to find ways to improve my learning.     − ? +
20e. I could give feedback to others in the same situation.     − ? +

     Total

# FEEDBACK

## Key Points

- Feedback involves a loop in which information about the effects of some action are fed back to the source of that action, so that it can be modified if necessary.

- The idea is so elegant and so powerful that it has spread to many fields, including teaching and training (where it used to be called 'knowledge of results'). Teachers/ trainers need feedback on the effects of their teaching; and learners need feedback on the effects of their learning. So there are two loops involved, and they overlap.

- One of the main sources of feedback is assessment (see Sections 21 and 22) but this is formal and may be too late to influence current learning. Students and trainees get informal or interim feedback in many other ways, including through small group work, and this helps shape their learning strategy. Even someone's reaction or body language can tell us something, though most feedback is more explicit than this. We learn very little from learning **tasks** (see Section 19) without some feedback on how we have performed.

- There are five conditions for effective feedback:

  ⇨ First, there has to be *somebody to give it*. This is usually the teacher/trainer, but we can get some useful feedback from our peers and even outsiders as well. Thus a supervisor or line manager might give us useful feedback on the training we are undergoing.

  ⇨ Second, the feedback has to be *informative*, and this usually means that it has to go into some detail. A single mark or tick does not tell us much; we need to know which elements of our learning worked well or not, and why.

  ⇨ Third, it has to be *timely*. With skills, this means immediate or rapid, otherwise the error may become in-built, and difficult to unlearn again. With other forms of learning, it needs to be reasonably soon, certainly soon enough for us to remember what we did and still be interested in changing it. Though a little delay can stimulate us to reflect on the work we have done, and try to evaluate it ourselves.

⇨ Fourth, there has to be someone to receive it. There is no point in people giving you feedback if you won't listen to them or *take it on board*. The problem is that we may see it as a criticism of ourselves, rather than our work.

⇨ Finally, there must be some possibility of *change*. It is frustrating to get feedback and then not be able to do anything about it because we cannot for some reason alter our response. There have to be ways forward, ways out.

✉ **Any problems with any of these?**

- On the whole, teachers and trainers are well aware of the importance of feedback. If they do not give adequate feedback it is probably because they haven't got enough time, and revert to bare marking or minimal responses, or the group is too large to give people the individual attention they deserve.

- Some staff – not many – are basically insensitive to people and don't take account of how students will react, sometimes because they are totally absorbed in their own subject or field. Some teachers/trainers also get into the habit of commenting only when something is wrong, and forget to give positive feedback as well. We need both, not least for our self-esteem.

- In the end, however, you have to develop some capacity to make your own judgements. We don't have someone looking over our shoulder all our life. Self-feedback may sound like a contradiction in terms, but in fact we use it all the time in everyday, **informal** learning.

✉ **Personal Notes**

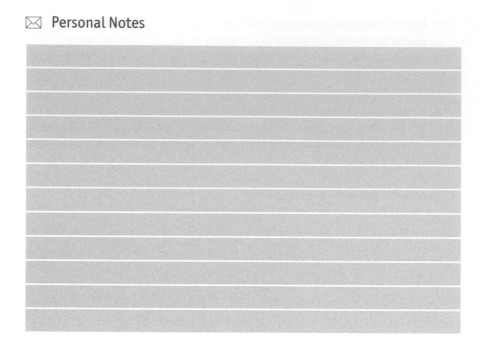

## Action

**If you aren't sure how well you are doing, ask**. You can sometimes do this at the end of a session, otherwise fix up an appointment. But it is probably best to wait until you are some way into the course, by which time the teacher/trainer will have had time to judge your progress. And you will have more experience to go on by then.

There may be statements in your **course material** about what is expected of you. Refer back to these and read them carefully; they will help you to evaluate your own progress.

**Before you get work back**, try to imagine the kinds of feedback you may get on it, both positive and critical. This will help you to develop your own sense of judgement. When you do get your work back

**go through it, don't just chuck it in a file**. There may be useful comments on it, which can help you adapt your approach next time. Teachers/trainers get irritated if they think you are not paying attention to what they have taken the trouble to write or say, and may not bother next time.

You can get **instant feedback** in group or tutorial sessions, as people (including the teacher/trainer) react to what you say. This is one reason for participating actively; you will learn from the experience. You can use it as an opportunity to test things out, as long as your performance is not being assessed at the time.

Some teachers are better at 'teaching subjects' than 'teaching students'. So if you get some **tactless feedback** from them, it is usually best to chalk it up to experience and get on with the job. However, if it becomes a continuing problem which is beginning to affect your motivation, you should try to talk it through with the person concerned, make them aware of its impact on you, and at least get it out of your system.

**Regular feedback** is more useful than leaving everything to the end, when it may be too late to alter your approach.

You can choose when you read written feedback. You don't have to absorb it all immediately; wait until you are in the **right frame of mind**.

With informal learning, feedback may be less explicit or obvious, certainly less formalised. You need to attune yourself to **look and listen** for it. It's probably there, but you have to become aware of it.

Don't allow yourself to be overwhelmed by **negative feedback**. The fact that you are on the course at all should mean that you lie somewhere within the necessary ability or achievement range.

The main danger is that you are either **over- or under-critical** of yourself, and sometimes people who work in isolation tend to these extremes. The best way to avoid these is to mix with other students or trainees, and you will probably get a more realistic sense how you stand from that.

## ✉ Feedback: what should I do?

# PART D: OUTCOMES

In this fourth part, we look at what comes out of your learning: not just your formal results in terms of assessment, but also what you have gained from it in terms of your own priorities and rewards. And we explore in what ways it has helped you to learn how to learn. There is also one final open section for you to add anything you want to the profile.

📖 When you have finished **Others** (Section 25), first look back at any of the other sections in Part D which you did not work through but which interest you.

📖 When you have done that, go directly to the **Profile** section (p. 174) near the end of the book and follow the instructions there.

PART D: OUTCOMES

# 21 Criteria
## what are they looking for?

**Sixth Form**

21a. I know what to expect in my assessments and exams.     − ? +
21b. I know what form my assessments and exams will take.     − ? +
21c. I know what they are looking for in the assessments and exams.     − ? +
21d. I know what will gain or lose me marks.     − ? +
21e. I know how to approach the questions.     − ? +

         Total

**Further Education**

21a. I know what to expect in my assessments.     − ? +
21b. I know what form my assessments will take.     − ? +
21c. I know what they are looking for in the assessments.     − ? +
21d. I know what will gain or lose me marks.     − ? +
21e. I know how to approach the questions and tasks.     − ? +

         Total

**Higher Education**

21a. I know what to expect in my assessments and exams.     − ? +
21b. I know the format of the assessments and exams.     − ? +
21c. I know what criteria will be used to judge me.     − ? +
21d. I know what will gain or lose me marks.     − ? +
21e. I know how to approach the questions.     − ? +

         Total

**Training and Development**

21a. I know what to expect in the training assessments.     − ? +
21b. I know what form the assessments will take.     − ? +
21c. I know what the assessment criteria will be.     − ? +
21d. I know what the assessors will be looking for.     − ? +
21e. I know how to approach the assessment tasks.     − ? +

         Total

**Informal Learning**

21a. I set myself the appropriate goals in my learning project.     − ? +
21b. I knew what I was trying to achieve.     − ? +
21c. I had realistic expectations of myself.     − ? +
21d. I knew how to assess my own learning.     − ? +
21e. I knew what standard I had reached.     − ? +

         Total

# CRITERIA

---

## Key Points

- This and the next section are about assessment. Most education and training is formally assessed. This section focuses on *what* is being assessed, and the next one on *how*. The term assessment here is being used generally to cover any form of coursework, exam, test, performance or project which is given a formal mark or grade.

- Assessment is important in itself, because it is the official result of your learning. In that sense, it is the bottom line, even if you have gained other things from your course.

- Assessment is also important because it affects the way you learn and the way you are trained and taught. It has a powerful magnetic influence on all that goes before, drawing everything towards it and sometimes even distorting it.

- However, not all courses and programmes are formally assessed, and you won't be if your case is one of the following:

    ⇨ many adult education courses don't involve any kind of test at the end, and people attend them simply out of interest, not because they want to get a piece of paper

    ⇨ a good deal of training and development takes place in short workshops or events which are too brief to assess

    ⇨ informal learning projects are by definition not assessed, although people may make their own judgements about how well they have succeeded.

📖 If you come into one of these categories, you can probably skip the rest of this section and Section 22, though they will still help you to think about learning in general terms.

- The fact remains that most education and training leads to some form of assessment. The key question here is: what is being assessed? what are the assessors looking for?

> 💣 **WARNING**: this is one aspect of learning where it is essential to consult your teacher. Assessment is geared to particular courses and only your teachers, lecturers or trainers are in a position to know what exactly is expected. Ask them and take careful account of their advice.

- Do you know what is expected of you? Do you know what the assessors or examiners actually want? Is it clear what criteria they will be using to judge you?

- If the initial objectives or outcomes of your course have been clearly spelled out, they will usually provide the answer, and you can simply refer back to them. However, such lists do not usually tell you what the priorities are, and if some objectives are actually more important than others, and might receive a heavier weighting.

- In other cases, the criteria may not be clear, either because people have not bothered to spell them out, or because it is very difficult to do so. The higher you go in education and training, the more complex things become, and it may be almost impossible to pin down and specify all the criteria that will be used. In this case you have to try to interpret what is likely to be required.

- It is important not only to understand what the content of the question will be, but what type of answer is required.* This is usually signalled by the verb in the question or the way it is asked. Verbs such as *name, list, define, state, give* or *describe* are asking you to reproduce the information you have learned in the form you learned it. Verbs such as *explain, show, compare, rank* or *apply* are asking you to manipulate or do something with that information. Verbs like *analyse, discuss, examine, explore* or *evaluate* go further still and require you to interpret and make judgements about it.

- Each field has a hierarchy of questions and tests going from simple to complex and if in doubt ask your teacher what is expected. The important thing is that you respond in the appropriate way to the kind of question that is being asked: a factual answer to an interpretative question (or vice versa) will not do. Skill learning has its own kind of hierarchy in terms of increasing complexity of operation, precision and speed. Arts such as music, painting and dance also have their own forms of progression, which are often quite difficult to define.

- All this raises the issue of level. Level is a very familiar term (NVQ levels, A level, undergraduate level 1, 2, 3, etc.) but it is actually quite complex.

## Level

Your course may consist of different levels or stages, so it is important to think about how one differs from another. Higher levels are differentiated from lower levels in two main ways:

1   MORE: there may simply be more content, wider scope, greater depth and detail.

2   DIFFERENT: they involve more complex kinds of learning in terms of the kinds of verbs listed earlier.

The second is trickier because it involves not only a quantitative increase in what you learn, but also a qualitative change of mental gear. Courses and subjects differ in the extent to which higher levels involve (1) and (2). Are the levels in your course more like

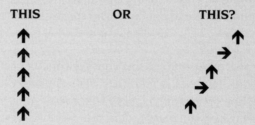

Higher level courses also tend to be more open-ended, require more interpretation of tasks, and assume greater autonomy and responsibility on your part.

- You also need to know what style of assessment response is needed. Are you expected to remember facts and details or not? What degree of precision is required? Do you need to come up with a definite conclusion or can you leave things open? Should you state both arguments and counter-arguments? Can you express your own views? Can you draw on your own experience?

- Not everything in the assessment process may be made explicit. There can be hidden criteria, or informal or unofficial things which are important. Some of these might relate to views and attitudes, which are sometimes not spelled out.

## ✉ Personal Notes

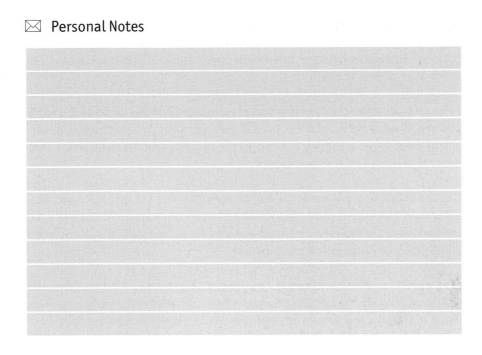

## Action

If you are not clear about the assessment criteria, **check your course handbook** or other documents to see if they are set out there. You may have missed them or not bothered to read them properly. Read them carefully again and think about what you will actually have to do. How do they relate to the content of your course?

If you are allowed access to them, get hold of **previous test or exam papers** and see what kinds of questions they ask, not just in terms of content but also the type and style of answer.

💣 **WARNING**: trying to work out what questions are likely to come up on the basis of what was asked last time and the times before (question-spotting) is a time-honoured but risky game, partly because there may be different examiners who start with a clean sheet, or the same ones who are playing the same game as you. You don't want your assessment to turn into a poker game of bluff and double-bluff, so it is important to revise and prepare an adequate range of answers. Teachers/trainers will advise.

If the assessment criteria are not clear or seem ambiguous, **ask your teachers/ trainers** to explain what they or the assessors are looking for. It is usually best to do this in a group, because different people will ask different questions from which everyone will benefit.

Ask your teacher/trainer if the assessment criteria will be **the same as the work you are already doing** on the course. If they are, what you are doing currently will be a good guide, and you can simply go on working in the same way. If they are not, find out how they will differ.

**Get feedback on early work**, so that you can take account of this in your final submission or assessment. This should happen anyway, but if not ask your teacher/trainer to look at a draft and give you some feedback on it. If you want clarification on some specific points, ask.

**Find someone who has already completed the course** or programme and who went through the same assessment process. Ask him or her what it was like. In particular, ask if there are any hidden criteria which are not spelled out and which you should be aware of. Any pitfalls? Points to emphasise?

Draw up a hit-list of **mistakes you should at all costs avoid making** or errors which will be heavily penalised. These will vary from course to course and sometimes even teacher to teacher, particularly if they have a bee in their bonnet about something. There may be formal marking schemes which will tell you how many marks are allocated to each task, and how you lose points on each one.

If there are no stated criteria, or if they are rather vague, **put yourself in the assessors' shoes**. What would **you** look for? How would you get at what people have learned? What kinds of questions would you ask? What kinds of test would you set? This is a useful exercise even if there are explicit criteria, since it makes you think hard about the whole assessment process.

If you are learning **informally** and independently, you have to **set your own criteria** anyway. How will you test yourself? How will you know when you have reached your target or goal? What standards will you apply to yourself?

## ✉ Criteria: what should I do?

# 22 Assessment
## methods and techniques

**Sixth Form**

22a. I know how to prepare for assessments and exams.     − ? +
22b. I have developed a good pattern of revision.     − ? +
22c. I have developed effective exam techniques.     − ? +
22d. I am good at managing assessment situations.     − ? +
22e. I think I will do myself justice in the assessments and exams.     − ? +

Total

**Further Education**

22a. I know how to prepare for assessment.     − ? +
22b. I have developed a good pattern of revision.     − ? +
22c. I have developed effective assessment techniques.     − ? +
22d. I am good at managing assessment situations.     − ? +
22e. I think I will do myself justice in the assessment.     − ? +

Total

**Higher Education**

22a. I know how to prepare for assessments and exams.     − ? +
22b. I have developed a good pattern of revision.     − ? +
22c. I have developed effective exam techniques.     − ? +
22d. I am good at managing assessment situations.     − ? +
22e. I think I will do myself justice in the assessments and exams.     − ? +

Total

**Training and Development**

22a. I know how to prepare for the training assessments.     − ? +
22b. I review what I have done regularly.     − ? +
22c. I know how to tackle each form of assessment.     − ? +
22d. I am good at managing assessment situations.     − ? +
22e. I think I will do myself justice in the assessments.     − ? +

Total

**Informal Learning**

22a. I knew how to assess myself.     − ? +
22b. I knew what tests to set myself.     − ? +
22c. I was an objective judge of my own performance.     − ? +
22d. I was good at managing my own performance.     − ? +
22e. I could assess someone else in the same situation.     − ? +

Total

# ASSESSMENT

## Key Points

- As well as knowing what you are going to be assessed on (see **Criteria**, Section 21) you need to know how. There are many different methods of assessment, and the first thing is to check the following list and ring the ones you will have to undergo:

  *classroom tests; quizzes; oral presentations; exercises; essays; reports; case studies; coursework assignments; multiple choice tests; true–false tests; completion tests; unseen exams, timed or untimed; open book exams; seen exams; oral exams; projects; portfolios; performances; role plays; simulations; practical demonstrations; interviews; on-the-job assessment. Any others?*

- Whichever type of assessment you have, you should be clear about the actual format. How much time will you have? Where will it take place? Under what conditions? What rules or restrictions will there be? How much choice will you have? There should be no surprises; you should know what you are in for.

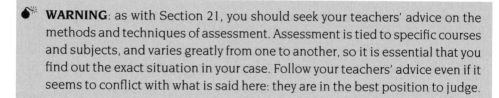

**WARNING**: as with Section 21, you should seek your teachers' advice on the methods and techniques of assessment. Assessment is tied to specific courses and subjects, and varies greatly from one to another, so it is essential that you find out the exact situation in your case. Follow your teachers' advice even if it seems to conflict with what is said here: they are in the best position to judge.

- You also need to think about how you will handle these situations. Each method of assessment creates its own particular demands. For example, written tests assume good writing skills and oral ones depend on verbal fluency. Some tests will require you to work fast, others will be more a matter of stamina. Others will involve performance in front of people. What techniques will you need to cope with these? How will you manage the particular pressures of each one?

- Some tests are sprung on people so that they have no chance to prepare, on the grounds that this gives a truer picture of what they have learned. But in most cases you will have some idea of what is coming. So you need to think about what kind of preparation or revision is needed. Do you know the time-scale for this? Will you get any special help or advice from staff?

- You also need to know what happens afterwards, as a result of the assessment. When do you get the results? What form do they take? What happens if you pass? What happens if you fail? Can you retake? If so, when?

## ✉ Personal Notes

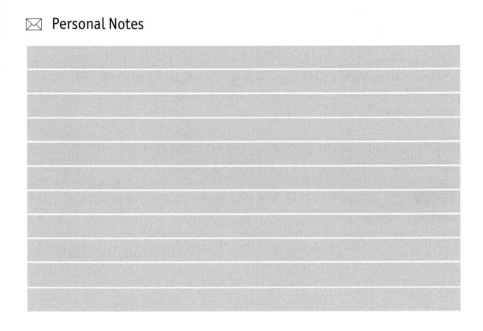

## Action

Try to build revision in as a regular part of your work rather than leaving it all to the end. Impose a 10% **revision tax** on yourself: one hour going over what you have covered for every ten hours of work (including class time). And watch out for tax avoidance . . . !

Even with this, you will probably need to **step up the revision** near the test or exam. Divide your revision into two categories: *standard* and *first class*. Standard revision is for all you have covered; first class is for the most difficult bits.

If you are revising over a period of weeks or months, **establish a pattern** which you can keep to. That will also make it easier for other people to adapt to, in terms of meal-times, going out, etc.

During your revision, **take breaks**. Don't run yourself into the ground. Do some exercises to relax tense muscles in the face, back and shoulders. Have a walk around.

Some people find that switching from one topic to another every so often helps them to **maintain concentration**. But people vary in their work styles, and you should find the pattern which suits you best.

Make use of **trial or mock assessments** if they exist. If you want to create your own mock assessments, set your questions or tasks first and leave them for a few days; then do them in realistic time and conditions and leave them another day or two before 'marking' them. That way, you will get a more detached view. Revising in **twos and threes** can be very useful, since you can test one another in turn, and also select topics to specialise in. As the saying goes, if you want to learn something, teach it!

If you become **anxious or panicky** in exams, it is probably the result of your earlier experiences coming back again (and that can happen even to adults after many years). You may have been 'conditioned' by past exams to react to the exam hall, the clock, the invigilator and so on. So it is the situation rather than you. Understanding this helps a bit. Some people go and see the exam hall beforehand, so that they 'pre-trigger' their emotional response, and get it over with before the actual occasion. You can also try '**replaying**' good exam experiences in your mind.

If you are worried about **forgetting** things, look at the **Memory** box.*

Find out about **stress management** techniques, such as breathing, exercises, visualisation, audio-tapes and aromatherapy. There are books and workshops on these. Some of them may work for you.

In verbal tests or exams, read the question. **Then read it again. Underline key words**.

In all subjects which require accuracy (maths, languages, technical fields) leave time to **check your answers** at the end. It is easy to lose marks through silly slips.

In subjects which require longer **essay-type answers**, you can **rough out a quick plan** first to see if you have enough material to answer the question. Then cross it out and begin. Also, leave some space at the end of each answer to add a few lines later.

There may be no choice in the **order of questions**, but if there is, you can decide whether to tackle the easiest one first (to give yourself a good start) or the most difficult one first (to get it over with).

Divide your time by the number of questions, or if they are unequal in length, budget for each type. But make sure to **leave enough time** for the last one(s); even if you answer the earlier ones really well, that is unlikely to compensate for not answering some questions at all.

In interviews or oral tests, **don't be rushed**. Answer at the normal pace, and give yourself time to think. You can sometimes **steer** the conversation towards the topics you are most familiar with.

You may get away without planning a short essay, but you won't with a project or longer piece of work. You have to **structure** it. If you write it in sections, make sure you build in any linking passages, so that it all hangs together.

**Portfolios** should be clearly organised with a table of contents and section headings; you don't want the assessors to get lost. And don't bulk out your file with unnecessary material, they will spot that a mile away.

On more advanced courses, if you have to give **references** in written work, make sure that they are accurate and in the correct format for your course (staff will advise). Give the references not only for everything you have quoted but also for any sources you have drawn on directly.

> **WARNING**: if in doubt, put the reference in, otherwise you may be accused of plagiarism (copying, stealing) and that's serious. And make sure quotations are indicated clearly as such.

Finally, remember that assessment results are **not as irrevocable as they used to be**. Nowadays there are many ways back – second chances or routes – in both education and training, and many adults have achieved later what they did not manage to do, for whatever reason, the first time round.

**Informal** learning differs in two ways. First, it involves self-assessment which is perhaps less stressful because you are in control, although some people are very stern judges of themselves. Second, the assessment is likely to be based on the actual performance of the task, rather than an artificial situation, and may be spread out over time. In that sense, it may not be a special event but rather the culmination of your work.

✉ **Assessment: what should I do?**

---

## Memory

Many learners worry about their memory, especially in assessment situations, so if you do, you're not alone. There are no magic solutions, but in terms of straightforward factual recall, here are four things you can try:

1  If there is a list or sequence, find a way, however trivial or accidental, of **linking** each item to the next one.

2  If there is no sequence, **group** the items (in threes, fours, fives, sixes) and learn them in those clusters rather than separately.

3  **Associate** an item with something else, such as a visual image or situation.

4  Find a general **acronym** (e.g. **SWOT** in **Course**, Section 1) or **pattern** that will embrace them all.

However, many memory questions go beyond simple recall, and involve relating what you have learned to some problem or task. The important thing here is to realise that you can **search** your memory. So, if it does not come up immediately on your mental screen, don't just give up. Try to get at it (if you have the time) as follows:

1   Think of something related to what you are trying to remember, and see if you can reach it indirectly through that. For example, you are unlikely to remember what you were doing this day last year, but you might be able to work it out by thinking about your weekly routine, where you were, any special events, etc.

2   Try using different pathways: for example, if you were trying to remember how many bridges there are in London, you could try thinking of their names, visualising their pictures, recollecting maps, remembering crossing them, comparing London with other cities, or guessing how few or how many there might be. We 'index' our memories in various ways, and if one way doesn't work, another might.

Memory is not an all-or-nothing process, and in some ways it is like problem-solving. Reflect on how you use it in everyday life, not just to recall names, faces and shopping lists, but also in interpreting new tasks and situations and drawing on past experience to inform the present. You will find that it is very much part of your perception, thinking and decision-making, rather than a distinct or separate entity on its own.

# 23  Reward
## what it means to you

**Sixth Form**

23a.  I can see the benefits of doing my subjects.       − ? +
23b.  I get satisfaction from the subjects I do.       − ? +
23c.  The teachers are positive about my work.       − ? +
23d.  My family are positive about my studies.       − ? +
23e.  I find my studies a rewarding experience.       − ? +

                                  Total

**Further Education**

23a.  I can see the benefits of doing my course.       − ? +
23b.  I get satisfaction from the work I do.       − ? +
23c.  The lecturers are positive about my work.       − ? +
23d.  Other people are positive about my education.       − ? +
23e.  Doing the course is a rewarding experience.       − ? +

                                  Total

**Higher Education**

23a.  I can see the benefits of doing my degree.       − ? +
23b.  I get satisfaction from my studies.       − ? +
23c.  The lecturers are positive about my work.       − ? +
23d.  Other people are positive about my studies.       − ? +
23e.  Doing the degree course is a rewarding experience.       − ? +

                                  Total

**Training and Development**

23a.  I can see how the training programme will benefit me.       − ? +
23b.  I get satisfaction from the work I do on the programme.       − ? +
23c.  I get a sense of achievement from my training.       − ? +
23d.  My organisation values the training I am doing.       − ? +
23e.  Doing the training programme is a rewarding experience.       − ? +

                                  Total

**Informal Learning**

23a.  I could see how my learning project would benefit me.       − ? +
23b.  I got satisfaction from the work I did on it.       − ? +
23c.  I derived a sense of achievement from my project.       − ? +
23d.  Other people valued what I learned from it.       − ? +
23e.  Doing my learning project was a rewarding experience.       − ? +

                                  Total

# REWARD

## Key Points

- One of the simplest but most powerful principles of learning is that we tend to learn what brings us pleasure or satisfaction. The opposite of this is that we usually try to avoid or suppress things that are painful in some way, or simply switch off if they are boring or unrewarding.

- So it is important to ask yourself if you find your course or project rewarding. What have you got from it? What will you gain by it? Do you enjoy it? Will you benefit from it in some way? There are different kinds of rewards.

   ⇨ Some are internal: a sense of satisfaction, achievement, pride or self-respect. The feeling that you have proved something to yourself, that you have done what you had it in you to do.

   ⇨ Other rewards are external: a qualification, a job, promotion, security, status, the respect or admiration of others. Often rewards are a mixture of internal and external and the balance may shift during the course or project itself.

   ⇨ Sometimes the rewards of a course are not the ones which the teachers/trainers have in mind. We might be bored by the subject but make new friends. We might find the content irrelevant but enjoy getting out of our house or job for a while. So when you think about rewards, reflect on the whole experience.

   ⇨ The importance of rewards is often clearest in their absence: the person who regularly comes bottom of the class; the student who gets poor marks; the teacher who only comments on work when there is something wrong with it; the trainee who feels isolated and unsupported; the adult learner whose hard work and achievements are ignored.

   ⇨ There may also be more subtle kinds of 'punishment'. The teacher or trainer puts you down. The others in the group exclude you. Your parents or peers are indifferent. Your friends do not think it is cool. Your partner is resentful. Your employer thinks training is a waste of time and money.

⇨ Without rewards, people begin to think: why should I bother? And if this experience is repeated again and again, they stop believing in themselves or lose all motivation. So they turn to other things which do give them some reward, and which mean more to them.

✉ **Cross-check your scores on Context (Section 11), Belief (Section 12), Motivation (Section 13) and Reward (Section 23). If they are similar, are there some common factors? If they differ, why is that?**

Context (   )          Belief (   )          Motivation (   )          Reward (   )

- What all this shows is the importance of attitudes and feelings. Learning is not just a thing of the mind. Even at a basic level, our attention and interest – what we notice or pick up – is affected by 'affective' (emotional) factors, as if our feelings subconsciously directed our mental radar towards what was important or rewarding. And the will to work at things and persevere depends heavily on what reinforces it, positively or negatively.

- Although work organisations and colleagues *should* value training and development, sometimes in reality they do not. They may resent covering for the absent person, be jealous of his or her prospects, or feel threatened by the new expertise he or she returns with. And when the trainee does come back, they can make it very difficult for her or him to apply or use what has been learned, and finds all sorts of ways of freezing them out.

- Reward and reinforcement can come from within the course or outside it. The best situation is when both are positive, but sometimes a positive course experience compensates for external discouragement, or vice versa. When both the course and the wider environment are negative, it takes a lot of determination and 'stickability' to keep going. But some people do, which only goes to show that internal, personal commitment can sometimes overcome enormous external obstacles.

Make notes on how any of this applies to you.

✉ Personal Notes

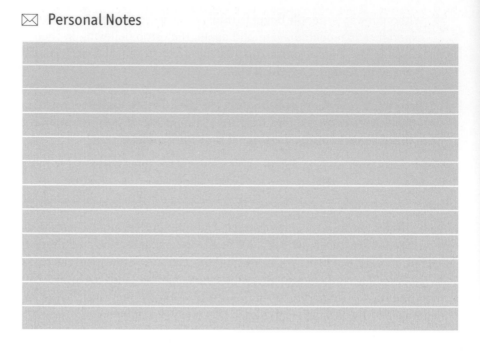

## Action

This is an aspect of learning which you can **think about yourself or talk over with others**, provided you know them quite well. People do not always want to share their feelings about these matters, so you may need to be tactful and supportive yourself.

Here are two simple exercises which you can do:

1  **List three learning experiences in the past** which you enjoyed and three which you did not. What were the common positive and negative factors?

2  **Make a balance sheet** of all the things which encourage you to learn at the moment, and all the ones which discourage you. What is the overall balance? Debit or credit?

Think about yourself. Are you the kind of person who depends a lot on **external support** and rewards, or the kind who does not seem to need them, and **goes their own way**? Have you always been the way you are? **Have you changed** in this respect?

Try to work out the balance between the **short term and the long term**. Perhaps you are struggling at the moment, but will it be worth it in the end? Teachers sometimes say that you will see the point of it all later, but that point may seem a long way off.

If you want to work out the consequences of your learning in a more systematic way, draw a **flow-chart** of what might happen (say) if you did well or poorly on your course or switched subjects or dropped out. **Informal** learners can do the same for their learning projects. Try to think of any side-effects or spin-offs as well. Leave the chart for a few days and you will probably add to it. Indeed, it may get quite messy in the end, but that doesn't matter as long as it helps you to think ahead and imagine the various 'scenarios' which might flow from your current decisions.

If you are feeling very down about the course or programme, go and talk to someone about it. **Better this than bottling it all up inside yourself**. When you do succeed, celebrate. **Give yourself a good time**. It is just as important to mark your achievements as to deal with the bad times. After all, learning is not easy, and you deserve it!

## ✉ Reward: what should I do?

# 24 Meta-learning
## learning how you learn

**Sixth Form**

24a. My studies have made me more aware of how I learn.    − ? +
24b. The experience has helped me to develop my study skills.    − ? +
24c. I know how to approach my studies better than I did.    − ? +
24d. I am more independent as a student than I was before.    − ? +
24e. I am a better judge of my own work than before.    − ? +

                   Total

**Further Education**

24a. The course has made me more aware of how I learn.    − ? +
24b. The course has helped me to develop my study skills.    − ? +
24c. I know how to approach my work better than I did.    − ? +
24d. I am more independent as a student than I was before.    − ? +
24e. I am a better judge of my own work than before.    − ? +

                   Total

**Higher Education**

24a. The course has made me more aware of how I learn.    − ? +
24b. The course has helped me to develop my study skills.    − ? +
24c. I know how to approach my studies better than I did.    − ? +
24d. I am more independent as a student than I was before.    − ? +
24e. I am a better judge of my own work than before.    − ? +

                   Total

**Training and Development**

24a. The programme has made me more aware of how I learn.    − ? +
24b. The programme has helped me to develop my learning skills.    − ? +
24c. I know how to approach my learning better than I did.    − ? +
24d. I am more independent as a learner than I was before.    − ? +
24e. I am a better judge of my own competence than before.    − ? +

                   Total

**Informal Learning**

24a. My project made me more aware of how I learn.    − ? +
24b. My project helped me to develop new learning skills.    − ? +
24c. I know how to approach my learning better than I did.    − ? +
24d. I am more independent as a learner now than I was before.    − ? +
24e. I am a better judge of my own progress than before.    − ? +

                   Total

# META-LEARNING

## Key Points

- This is the final heading because it is the one to which all the others lead in the end. Meta-learning means learning about learning. Has doing your course or project helped you to learn how to learn?

- At the simplest level, it may have given you some new study skills. For example, you might be better now at searching for information and boiling it down in the form of notes or summaries. You may have developed better listening or reading skills. You might be more fluent at writing or communicating with others. Can you handle exams or assessments better now?

- Have you added some new skills altogether, which you did not possess before? Computing? Retrieving information? Giving presentations? Planning projects?

- You may also have become better at sizing up the learning situation you are in, and the demands it places on you. Better at understanding the kinds of tasks or assignments you are faced with, at defining or tackling problems. Better at 'reading' situations in the classroom or group, and picking up cues or signals. Better at relating to the people around you. More 'coursewise'.

- Developing your learning skills and interpreting the learning situation are important aspects of *meta-learning*, but there is a third and even more basic way of looking at it. Have you actually begun to teach yourself? Are you better able to take over some of the things that teachers/trainers do for you and carry them out yourself? This doesn't mean that you don't need the teacher or trainer at all, but that you become more independent or autonomous as a learner.

- There are several sides to this independence:

    ⇨ One is the capacity to set your own goals or decide your own direction, without always having someone to tell you what to do.

    ⇨ Another is the capacity to motivate yourself and create your own momentum.

⇨  A third is the ability to organise yourself, to get it together.

⇨  A fourth is the capacity to judge your own work and progress. This last is perhaps the most difficult but most important.

•  Being able to analyse your learning is only half the story; the other half is to change it, and that is often easier said than done. You should not expect overnight miracles. Learning to learn is a long-term process. But often it is good to start with smaller, more practical changes which can make an immediate difference. That way, you feel you are making headway, which then gives you confidence to tackle the bigger issues.

How does this apply to you? You may not even have been aware of your own 'meta-learning' because you were so involved in the course or project itself. But now you can stand back from the experience and reflect on it. Has it changed you? Are you a different student/trainee/person now from the one who embarked on it all?

## ✉ Personal Notes

# Action

**Reflect and discuss.**

You need to take time out from whatever you are learning or studying to think about how you are doing and how it is going. Even if you feel under pressure of work and deadlines, stand back occasionally and try to get your distance. **Reflecting on your learning** is probably the single most important thing you can do to improve it.

One useful way is to keep a **diary**. As was said earlier, don't make this too much of a chore, otherwise you'll soon abandon it.

You can also try to draw a **pen-portrait** of yourself as a student/trainee/learner. How do others see you? How do you come across? What are your main strengths and weaknesses? (Do it with an actual picture or caricature if you want!)

Imagine that you have to write a **letter** to someone who is just coming on the course or embarking on their project, giving them some basic advice. What would you say? What are the essential survival skills? What do you wish you had known?

You can also **discuss** your learning with others. You might be doing this anyway as part of an organised part of your course. More likely it is something you will do informally on the phone or with a few friends over a coffee.

Sometimes the people on a course create a kind of '**shadow course**' in which they carry on a running discussion of the course itself, outside the class. Sharing experiences and problems with others is one of the most valuable forms of meta-learning. At a minimum, you will probably find that you are not as alone as you thought.

You can structure your group discussion if you wish. One way is to draw a box in the centre of a large piece of paper, and then divide the space outside it into the number of people in the group (not more than five or six). Put all the **things you experience in common** inside the box, and all the **ways in which your experiences differ** in the segments outside (there may be some argument about this). Then talk about both.

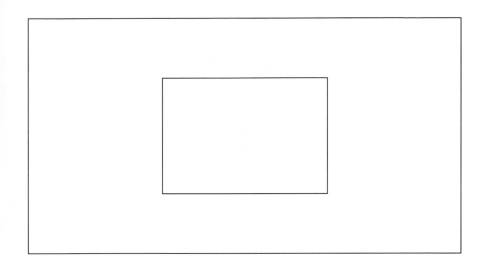

If you are interested in exploring your and other people's **learning styles**, use the special box below. Learning styles refer to ways in which individuals are consistent in themselves but different from one other in how they process information and approach learning tasks.* Each style forms a continuum on which you should place yourself somewhere, not necessarily at either end. Note that one end is not necessarily better than the other. While learning styles offer a useful framework for reflecting on your learning, they should not be regarded as fixed or given. Ask yourself first, to what extent your style is consistent or depends on the task/situation, second, whether it has changed over time, and third, whether you could alter it if you wanted or needed to. It may also be useful to distinguish between preferred styles and adopted styles. Another question is whether it is better to try to match your style to the style of the subject and the teaching, or whether you might learn from a mismatch which would challenge you to work in a different way.

You might also want to explore ideas about **different kinds of ability**. For example, one job classification scheme rates each job out of 10 in terms of work with *Ideas, People* and *Things*.* So for example a care worker might score more highly on the second than the other two (3–8–4?) a mechanic more highly on the third (5–3–9?) and a teacher more highly on the first two (8–8–3?) though that could depend on the kind of teaching and indeed teacher. This sort of exercise can lead to some interesting arguments about the real nature of the job, and whether it is changing; for example secretarial work would rate higher on *Things* (office technology) than it did in the early 1980s. If you do a job (or are thinking about a career) try classifying it in this way, and see if that matches your own abilities and preferences.

There is also a lot of interest currently in the idea of **multiple intelligences**.*
Some writers argue that instead of having a single measure of intelligence such
as IQ, it is more useful to distinguish between different kinds of intelligence
e.g. logical-mathematical, linguistic, spatial, bodily-kinaesthetic, musical,
interpersonal and so on. As with learning styles, this is a complex and much
disputed area, for example in terms of the distinctness of the different forms
of intelligence, how we know when to use or deploy them, and whether there
is not some common factor such as speed or problem-solving in them all.
However, the idea raises interesting questions about the ways people see
themselves as learners, and what they think they are good at. As a start, think
about the different areas of your life (home, job, leisure, education and so on)
and what kinds of ability or talents you bring to each of them. Are some of
these abilities stronger or more developed than others? Do you need to make
any strategic decisions about the direction of your learning?

---

## Learning Styles

1 **Convergent/Divergent**: tendency to think logically and systematically,
or in a more open-ended, imaginative way

    Convergent     x    x    x    x    x    Divergent

2 **Concrete/Abstract**: preference for practical or concrete tasks and
problems, or more theoretical, conceptual or abstract ones

    Concrete     x    x    x    x    x    Abstract

3 **Reflective/Active**: preference for standing back, analysing and
reflecting, or learning through doing and direct involvement

    Reflective     x    x    x    x    x    Active

4 **Serialist/Holist**: tendency to work step by step or stage by stage, or to
begin with the whole picture and then get down to details

    Serialist     x    x    x    x    x    Holist

5 **Optimiser/Satisficer**: tendency to do things as well as possible, or to
judge what is appropriate to meet the needs of the situation

    Optimiser     x    x    x    x    x    Satisficer

6 **Analytic/Impressionistic**: tendency to analyse or break down things into their elements or parts, or to absorb and respond to the overall, total impression

    Analytic       x     x     x     x     x    Impressionistic

7 **Includer/Excluder**: tendency to draw boundaries widely and include elements, or to draw them tightly and exclude them

    Includer       x     x     x     x     x    Excluder

8 **Planner/Improviser**: preference for planning ahead and having a clear structure, as against working in a more spontaneous, opportunistic or incremental way

    Planner       x     x     x     x     x    Improviser

9 **Single-tasking/Multi-tasking**: preference for working on one task or activity at a time, or working on concurrent or alternating tasks

    Single-tasking   x     x     x     x     x    Multi-tasking

10 **Sprinter/Long-distance runner**: preference for working in intensive spurts or bursts, or adopting and maintaining a steady, sustainable pace

    Sprinter       x     x     x     x     x    Long-distance

11 **Risk-taker/Risk-avoider**: tendency to experiment and take risks, or to choose a more secure and predictable course of action

    Risk-taker     x     x     x     x     x    Risk-avoider

12 **Individualist/Interactionist**: preference for working independently on one's own at one's own pace, or for working in, with and through a group

    Individualist    x     x     x     x     x    Interactionist

## ✉ Meta-learning: what should I do?

# 25 Others

The 24 sections in this book have covered the main aspects of your learning situation. However, learning is a very individual business, and it is difficult to cater for every person and every context. This last section encourages you to add one or more headings of your own if you wish.

Try to think of at least ONE more factor that affects your learning, positively or negatively, which has not been covered already. You may need to look back at some of the previous sections to check this, and it might also be useful to talk it over with someone else if you can; different people are likely to come up with different headings. Don't worry about whether you should include it or not; if it is important to you, it's important. Here are some examples, but don't feel limited by them:

*Age; gender; time; health; disability; money; emotional factors; social life; prejudice; change of environment; relevance to job; relevance to personal goals; sense of achievement; sense of excitement; relationships; family commitments; studying part-time; being valued for oneself; curiosity; change from school to college/university; change of job; change of role or position; change of country.*

Make some notes on it and give it a plus or minus rating (from −5 to +5). Then go directly to the **Profile**. And if you want to add others, there is room to draw more boxes there.

## ⊠ Personal Notes

| HEADING: | RATING: |
|---|---|
| | |
| | |
| | |
| | |
| | |
| | |
| | |
| | |
| | |
| | |

Now think about the implications of this for future action.

## ⊠ Others: what should I do?

Notes and Further Reading

Tips for the Terrified
computing, languages, maths, presentations, writing

Notes for Staff

Study Skills Index

Profile and Action Plan

# Notes and Further Reading

This book is based on a three-dimensional model of teaching and training which has been set out in theoretical terms in Squires, G. (1999) *Teaching as a Professional Discipline*, London: Falmer. Essentially, this book takes the teaching/learning 'functions' listed on one dimension of that model and uses them as the basis for each of the 24 sections (some functions have been subdivided). That model in turn derives from a general theory of professional work which can be applied to other professional fields: for an application to management, see Squires, G. (2001) 'Management as a professional discipline', *Journal of Management Studies* 38(4), 473–487. The analysis of informal learning here also reflects a previous research report on the topic: see Gear, J., McIntosh, A. and Squires, G. (1994) *Informal Learning in the Professions*, Hull: University of Hull Department of Continuing Education. Most of the ideas and sources on which this book draws can be found in the above, but the following relate to specific references in the text which readers may want to pursue.

p. 10  The phrase 'hidden curriculum' refers to all those aspects of a course or programme which are not explicitly or officially spelled out. Sometimes 'hidden' implies concealed, but more often it points merely to the existence of the tacit element of teaching and learning. See the relevant chapters in Meighan, R. and Siraj-Blatchford, I. (1997) A *Sociology of Educating*, 3rd edn, London: Cassell. One also sometimes finds the phrase 'inner curriculum' which refers to the internal goals and plans which learners may have, something which is by no means confined to informal learning.

p. 25  The distinction between optimising and satisficing was first drawn by Herbert Simon in an organisational context, with the latter having negative connotations of administrative convenience. See Simon, H. (1976) *Administrative Behavior*, 3rd edn, London: Collier Macmillan. My use here is obviously different, with no preference for one or the other.

p. 36  For a useful summary of the implications of the main learning theories, see Hartley, J. (1998) *Learning and Studying: a research perspective*, London: Routledge. For a more detailed account see any standard textbook such as Biehler, R. F. and

Snowman, J. (1993) *Psychology Applied to Teaching*, 7th edn, Boston, MA: Houghton Mifflin. On the whole, however, learning is now seen in a more contextualised way, and there is less emphasis on formal theory than there used to be.

p. 44 The main exponent of social learning theory which is the basis of modelling is Albert Bandura: see Bandura, A. (1986) *Social Foundations of Thought and Action*, Englewood Cliffs, NJ: Prentice-Hall.

p. 47 There has been a good deal of research on self-directedness in adult learning, though my spectrum here is slightly different and not confined to adults. See Tennant, M. (1997) *Psychology and Adult Learning*, 2nd edn, London: Routledge, for this and other aspects of adult learning.

p. 51 The main author in the field of emotional intelligence is Daniel Goleman: see Goleman, D. (1998) *Working with Emotional Intelligence*, London: Bloomsbury.

p. 63 For an anthropological perspective on disciplinary cultures in higher education see Becher, T. (1989) *Academic Tribes and Territories*, Milton Keynes: Open University Press.

p. 74 For a good introduction to self-belief and similar topics, see the chapter on 'The Self' in Fontana, D. (1995) *Psychology for Teachers*, 3rd edn, London: Macmillan/BPS Books. The importance of self-esteem and a sense of self-efficacy is also an important theme in some management writing.

p. 80 The different theories of motivation which developed historically, and which one finds in any standard textbook, have now tended to give way to a more contextualised and eclectic approach, which is reflected in this book. The picture is muddier but perhaps more realistic.

p. 83 The distinction between deep and surface learning was first drawn by the Swedish researcher Ferens Marton, but has since generated a good deal of research in higher education in the UK and Australia. See for example Ramsden, P. (1992) *Learning to Teach in Higher Education*, London: Routledge. One interesting question is how far these strategies are a response to the learning environment, including teaching style and assessment.

p. 101 The five stages in skill learning set out here are simplified. For a detailed account of the processes of skill learning see Patrick, J. (1992) *Training: research and practice*, London: Academic Press. A lot depends on the nature of the skill being learned.

p. 133 Current practice in assessment is still influenced (sometimes unknowingly) by Bloom's *Taxonomy* in this respect, despite the various criticisms levelled at it over the years, in particular the problems of devising a 'subject free' hierarchy. See Bloom, B. S. *et al.* (eds) (1956) *Taxonomy of Educational Objectives, Handbook 1: cognitive domain*, London: Longmans. There is a companion volume on the affective domain edited by D. R. Krathwohl.

p. 142 The literature on memory is vast, complex and interesting. Like learning, one more recent trend has been to move away from laboratory settings to study memory in its everyday manifestations. For a general account, see Baddeley, A. (1997) *Human Memory: theory and practice*. Hove: Psychology Press.

p. 157 This is a very contentious topic, with disagreements about the basis, nature and number of learning or cognitive styles. The literature tends to deal with specific styles and ranges from the popular to the highly technical, but there is a useful introductory chapter on individual differences in Hartley, J. (1998) *Learning and Studying: a research perspective*, London: Routledge. For a detailed discussion, see Riding, R. and Rayner, S. (1998) *Cognitive Styles and Learning Strategies*, London: David Fulton. The list here is an eclectic one, and includes dimensions which do not stem from mainstream educational and psychological research but which I have found useful with students in practice, as long as the dimensions are treated with some scepticism and merely as tools for thinking about one's approach to learning.

p. 157 This scheme of job classification was originally developed by the US Department of Labor.

p. 158 Although the idea of the plurality of intelligence is by no means new, the best known modern exponent is Howard Gardner, any of whose books will provide an interesting, if debatable, account. The attraction of this work to many is that it promises a more pluralistic appreciation of human abilities, though that may be sharply limited in practice by the way society currently rewards different kinds of work and talent. At the theoretical level, there has been a long-running unity/plurality debate in the field, which is not yet resolved. Robert Sternberg's work in this field is equally important, though more difficult to summarise, and he has also contributed more recently to the literature on learning styles: see Sternberg, R. (1997) *Thinking Styles*, Cambridge: Cambridge University Press.

# Tips for the Terrified

## computing, languages, maths, presentations, writing

Some people have a real phobia about the above areas, either because of bad experiences at school, or because they have never done them before. Here, if you need them, are a few basic tips to get you started. Beyond that, seek help from your teacher/trainer or find out if there are any courses or workshops you can enrol on. This is only a beginning . . .

## Computing

- Find someone to show you. Manuals and help-screens are often as complicated as the program itself, though your institution may have produced a simple guide.
- Ask him or her to slow down. Computer people tend to do things too quickly.
- Make sure you can get out of situations as well as into them. Always ask: how do I get back to where I was?
- Keep a little notebook beside you and write down your own instructions. That way you will understand them properly.
- Practise each operation two or three times to make sure you can really perform it.
- Take your time. Speed is not important.
- Don't worry, you won't break it.
- Work at it regularly, otherwise you will forget.

## Languages

- Do a little often rather than a lot occasionally.
- Take risks. You will make mistakes but you will learn from them.
- Listen to tapes to get your ear attuned.
- Read vocab lists three times: top down, bottom up and top down again. Then test yourself. If the list has more than 10–12 items, divide it in half and do the same.

- Try imagining *one* change when you write or speak a sentence (present to past, statement to question, singular to plural, male to female, different adjective, etc). That way you will learn how to vary the patterns.
- Keep an error book. Note down any repeated mistakes you make and cross them out when you no longer do.
- Check your work before you hand it in.
- Have a go.

## Maths

- In maths, if you do it right, you get it right.
- Make sure you understand every little step. Don't skip or gloss over anything.
- Make sure you are doing things in the right order.
- Keep an error log of the mistakes you make. Cross them out when you no longer do.
- Try to grasp the underlying principles rather than just jumping through hoops. If you don't, ask, and if you still don't, ask again.
- Understand the purpose of it. Otherwise maths is just meaningless procedures.
- Take your time. Except in some exams, speed is not important.
- Check your workings. It is easy to make a slip.
- Get a feel for the solution. Does it look right?

## Presentations

- Don't put too much in. Maximum three key points in five minutes, five in ten minutes.
- Keep a little bit in reserve near the end in case you look like running out.
- List your main points at the start, preferably on a transparency; make the writing large enough; if you can't write clearly, print.
- Speak, don't read. Have clear, large notes you can see at a glance, maybe on a card.
- Project your voice and don't drop it at the ends of sentences.
- Look at people, and not just the front row.
- If you want to get a discussion going, present conflicting views.
- Provide a handout at the end that summarises it all.
- Have your final sentence worked out so that you exit gracefully.

# Writing

- Make an outline of your essay/assignment first and leave it for a day or so.
- Say what you are going to say in the introduction.
- Build up your writing in paragraphs. State your main point at the beginning and then develop it through examples, evidence, questions, arguments and counter-arguments.
- Don't feel that the writing must be complicated just because it is an essay. Think: how would I explain this to someone?
- Don't let your sentences get too long or you may lose track of them.
- If you are unsure about spelling, buy a compact dictionary and check.
- Read a lot. It helps all other communication skills.
- Don't try to come to a firm conclusion if there isn't one.

# Notes for Staff

This book is designed for students and trainees to work through on their own, but it can be used in organised groups or classes as well. Indeed, this may have advantages in some circumstances in terms of relating the book to the current course or subject and in supporting less motivated or confident learners. You will be in the best position to judge how to use the book, but here are some general guidelines:

- The book should be used when participants are already some way into a course, or near the end of it, not at the beginning when they won't yet have enough experience of it to respond to many parts of the questionnaires.

- It can be used with mixed groups from different subjects or courses, as long as the areas are not too dissimilar. The variety should throw up interesting comparisons.

- Ideally, the work should be spread over two or three sessions in order to allow time for reflection. Where it has to be completed in one day, for example in a training workshop, build in good breaks so that people have plenty of opportunities to chat informally.

- Doing some of the work in subgroups of three to five not only increases the amount of interaction but also gives participants more security. They can speak in the name of the group rather than laying themselves on the line. And they can say some things in the relative privacy of the group which they might not want to voice in front of you and everyone else.

- If you want people to do some preparatory work to save time, ask them to complete Part A before coming. Debrief them on that before moving on to the rest, making sure they are clear about both the procedures and the purpose of the exercise.

- There is potentially a good deal of reading in the text, and some people will find that too much. An alternative is to complete the questionnaires and fill in the Profile first. Then collate the results and see if there are any general patterns. If so, you can lead the group through the sections, beginning perhaps with the least problematic and spending most time on those which produce the lowest scores.

- In exploring any general patterns, think about the extent to which each aspect is within or outside participants' control, whether the issues are mainly cognitive or affective, and whether people attribute them to themselves or their environment.

- If you want to go for a 'light touch' approach, introduce the book to the learners, ask them to organise themselves in small groups and let them get on with it. It may be useful to have a general, debriefing session when they have all finished.

- The process will throw up criticisms of courses and staff, and you need to establish clear ground-rules about this, otherwise participants may hesitate to voice their real feelings. Your colleagues will need to agree to these ground-rules too. Learner development (such as this) has potential implications for staff development, curriculum development and organisation development.

- Assessment (Sections 21 and 22) is often something that produces strong reactions, and you need to be prepared for these and think through the possible issues in advance.

- Many of the activities in the book can be adapted for group use, but feel free to devise some of your own if you wish. And if you want to integrate them with material from other sources, particularly if it is subject-related, do so.

- One advantage of using the book as part of a formal programme is that you can build it into the ongoing process. It is important that the analysis here is integrated into the overall system of learner support and development, not treated as a one-off exercise. Individual action plans can be pursued, and it may be useful to have a general follow-up session some time later.

- The most important thing in the end is people's attitude to their own learning. The book should not be seen merely as a tool-kit or a rigid set of external prescriptions, but as the Preface puts it, the basis for an internal conversation, and one that will go on well into the future. Above all, people need to engage with their own learning and take ownership of it.

# Study Skills Index

This book has been about understanding your learning, not just skills and techniques. However, although such practical skills are not enough on their own, they do form an essential part of the way you learn and you may want to refer back to them. You can find something about them on the pages below.

# Profile and Action Plan

## Instructions

📖 Before you complete the profile, make sure that you have read at least 12 of the sections in the book, and preferably more. These should consist of the ones which you worked through because your score was less than +3, and any others which you looked back at when you finished each part. Anything less than 12 will not give you a detailed enough picture of how you learn.

📖 Starting from the centre of the profile, shade in each line as far as your plus or minus score. (If you have 0 on some lines, shade only that column.) In this way, you will be able to see the shape of your learning profile easily.

Remember that the important thing is not to get a positive or negative profile but to **understand the reasons why**: only in that way can you begin to manage your learning. Most people come out with a **mixture of plus and minus scores**, so don't be surprised if your profile looks like that. Perhaps at this point too you can think about whether you have been too lenient or severe on yourself. Having finished the whole exercise, would you still give yourself the same scores?

Remember also that **the situation may change**, because your course/project changes or you change. The profile is not just of you, but you in your current context. The kind of course or learning you are doing, the people you are doing it with, the place you are doing it in and the staff who are teaching/training you, will all be reflected in the profile. So this is not some fixed, external print-out, but rather the basis for some **personal reflection or conversation with your friends or colleagues**.

When you have looked at your profile, make notes on the following questions:

✉ **Is it you? Really you?**

☒  Has it changed? (Over the last year?)

<br>

☒  Is it likely to change? (Over the next year?)

<br>

There are **three copies** of the profile in case you need or want to complete it more than once at different times or for different areas of learning. (You may even need to use different versions of the questionnaires.) This is a useful thing to do, since it will give you some sense of how your learning is changing and evolving over time. Unless your situation has altered dramatically, it is probably best to wait about a year before working through the book again. That should give you enough distance from the first time to allow you to compare your previous responses with your new ones. Use the margins to enter your responses or write your new notes if you haven't rubbed the old ones out.

📖 On the back of each profile there is an **Action Plan**. When you have analysed the profile and your reaction to it, turn over the page and write down the key points in your action plan, dividing them into short term (over the next few weeks) and long term (over the next few months or year). You will probably need to refer back to the **What should I do?** boxes you filled in for the relevant sections.

📖 You can show this Action Plan to others and discuss it with them if you wish, but the most important thing is to treat it as a kind of **contract** with yourself. Try to fulfil it, and check back occasionally to see if you are.

And whatever kind of learning you are involved in, good luck with it!

# PROFILE

| | −5 | −4 | −3 | −2 | −1 | 0 | +1 | +2 | +3 | +4 | +5 |
|---|---|---|---|---|---|---|---|---|---|---|---|
| 1 Course | | | | | | | | | | | |
| 2 Induction | | | | | | | | | | | |
| 3 Resources | | | | | | | | | | | |
| 4 Managing | | | | | | | | | | | |
| 5 Teaching | | | | | | | | | | | |
| 6 Learning | | | | | | | | | | | |
| 7 Modelling | | | | | | | | | | | |
| 8 Support | | | | | | | | | | | |
| 9 Interaction | | | | | | | | | | | |
| 10 Environment | | | | | | | | | | | |
| 11 Context | | | | | | | | | | | |
| 12 Belief | | | | | | | | | | | |
| 13 Motivation | | | | | | | | | | | |
| 14 Foundations | | | | | | | | | | | |
| 15 Orientation | | | | | | | | | | | |
| 16 Input | | | | | | | | | | | |
| 17 Understanding | | | | | | | | | | | |
| 18 Enquiry | | | | | | | | | | | |
| 19 Tasks | | | | | | | | | | | |
| 20 Feedback | | | | | | | | | | | |
| 21 Criteria | | | | | | | | | | | |
| 22 Assessment | | | | | | | | | | | |
| 23 Reward | | | | | | | | | | | |
| 24 Meta-learning | | | | | | | | | | | |
| 25 Others | | | | | | | | | | | |

# ACTION PLAN

A. Short term (the next few weeks)

1
.................................................................................................
.................................................................................................
.................................................................................................

2
.................................................................................................
.................................................................................................
.................................................................................................

3
.................................................................................................
.................................................................................................
.................................................................................................

B. Long term (three to twelve months)

1
.................................................................................................
.................................................................................................
.................................................................................................

2
.................................................................................................
.................................................................................................
.................................................................................................

3
.................................................................................................
.................................................................................................
.................................................................................................

# PROFILE

|  | −5 | −4 | −3 | −2 | −1 | 0 | +1 | +2 | +3 | +4 | +5 |
|---|---|---|---|---|---|---|---|---|---|---|---|
| 1 Course | | | | | | | | | | | |
| 2 Induction | | | | | | | | | | | |
| 3 Resources | | | | | | | | | | | |
| 4 Managing | | | | | | | | | | | |
| 5 Teaching | | | | | | | | | | | |
| 6 Learning | | | | | | | | | | | |
| 7 Modelling | | | | | | | | | | | |
| 8 Support | | | | | | | | | | | |
| 9 Interaction | | | | | | | | | | | |
| 10 Environment | | | | | | | | | | | |
| 11 Context | | | | | | | | | | | |
| 12 Belief | | | | | | | | | | | |
| 13 Motivation | | | | | | | | | | | |
| 14 Foundations | | | | | | | | | | | |
| 15 Orientation | | | | | | | | | | | |
| 16 Input | | | | | | | | | | | |
| 17 Understanding | | | | | | | | | | | |
| 18 Enquiry | | | | | | | | | | | |
| 19 Tasks | | | | | | | | | | | |
| 20 Feedback | | | | | | | | | | | |
| 21 Criteria | | | | | | | | | | | |
| 22 Assessment | | | | | | | | | | | |
| 23 Reward | | | | | | | | | | | |
| 24 Meta-learning | | | | | | | | | | | |
| 25 Others | | | | | | | | | | | |

# ACTION PLAN

## A. Short term (the next few weeks)

1
........................................................................................................................................................................
........................................................................................................................................................................
........................................................................................................................................................................

2
........................................................................................................................................................................
........................................................................................................................................................................
........................................................................................................................................................................

3
........................................................................................................................................................................
........................................................................................................................................................................
........................................................................................................................................................................

## B. Long term (three to twelve months)

1
........................................................................................................................................................................
........................................................................................................................................................................
........................................................................................................................................................................

2
........................................................................................................................................................................
........................................................................................................................................................................
........................................................................................................................................................................

3
........................................................................................................................................................................
........................................................................................................................................................................
........................................................................................................................................................................

# PROFILE

| | −5 | −4 | −3 | −2 | −1 | 0 | +1 | +2 | +3 | +4 | +5 |
|---|---|---|---|---|---|---|---|---|---|---|---|
| 1 Course | | | | | | | | | | | |
| 2 Induction | | | | | | | | | | | |
| 3 Resources | | | | | | | | | | | |
| 4 Managing | | | | | | | | | | | |
| 5 Teaching | | | | | | | | | | | |
| 6 Learning | | | | | | | | | | | |
| 7 Modelling | | | | | | | | | | | |
| 8 Support | | | | | | | | | | | |
| 9 Interaction | | | | | | | | | | | |
| 10 Environment | | | | | | | | | | | |
| 11 Context | | | | | | | | | | | |
| 12 Belief | | | | | | | | | | | |
| 13 Motivation | | | | | | | | | | | |
| 14 Foundations | | | | | | | | | | | |
| 15 Orientation | | | | | | | | | | | |
| 16 Input | | | | | | | | | | | |
| 17 Understanding | | | | | | | | | | | |
| 18 Enquiry | | | | | | | | | | | |
| 19 Tasks | | | | | | | | | | | |
| 20 Feedback | | | | | | | | | | | |
| 21 Criteria | | | | | | | | | | | |
| 22 Assessment | | | | | | | | | | | |
| 23 Reward | | | | | | | | | | | |
| 24 Meta-learning | | | | | | | | | | | |
| 25 Others | | | | | | | | | | | |

# ACTION PLAN

## A.  Short term (the next few weeks)

1

2

3

## B.  Long term (three to twelve months)

1

2

3